Praise for *TeenVes*

Named one of the "Best Investment Books of 2002

"*TeenVestor®* is another excellent resource for learning not only the basics of investing in stocks, mutual funds, and IRAs, but also the workings of the economy   —*Barron's*

"Written especially for teenagers, although it's actually a good basic resource for any age . . . Good, solid (not dumbed-down) explanations of investment basics. I like this book because it encourages parents to come along for the ride and learn about investing, too."   —Money.com

"In-depth and sophisticated . . . [*TeenVestor®*] doesn't assume its readers have had prior exposure to investing or easy access to money . . . Teens and parents will appreciate the detailed treatment of investing strategies."

—Morningstar.com

"The authors explain the basics of investing . . . how to understand the stock market and how to evaluate and choose stocks for the long-term . . . Accurate, objective, and helpful."   —*School Library Journal*

"Psst. Find this website on the Internet and bookmark it. *TeenVestor.com*. Just don't let anyone know you're using it. It's supposed to be for kids. If you want to learn about investing, this is the place to go. It's for teens, but if you won't tell, we won't either. This is good stuff."   —*Independent Tribune*

"Both the book and the website are clearly laid out . . . Most teens are not old enough to invest through a regular investment account, so there's a chapter going through the options open to parents of teens, such as custodial accounts and IRAs. Good information in an accessible, and unlike many books aimed toward the younger market, unpatronizing manner."   —FinancialFinesse.com

"A well-organized, easy-to-understand format . . . should be required reading for all high school students and their parents."

—Peter E. Breen, Executive Vice President, Fahnstock

MAD
cASH

A First Timer's Guide to Investing
$30 to $3,000

By Emmanuel Modu
and Andrea Walker

A PERIGEE BOOK

P

A Perigee Book
Published by The Berkley Publishing Group
A division of Penguin Group (USA) Inc.
375 Hudson Street
New York, New York 10014

First edition: August 2003

Library of Congress Cataloging-in-Publication Data
Modu, Emmanuel.
    Mad cash: a first timer's guide to investing $30 to $3000 / Emmanuel
Modu and Andrea Walker.
        p. cm.
Includes index.
    ISBN 0-399-52896-2
    1. Investments—Handbooks, manuals, etc.   I. Walker, Andrea.   II. Title

HG4527.M57 2003
332.63'2—dc21

                                                           2003048655

Printed in the United States of America

10 9 8 7 6 5 4 3 2 1

Mad Cash is dedicated to our agent, Jane Jordan Browne of Multimedia Product Development, who left this earth on February 27, 2003. Jane, thanks for 12 years of a great partnership—we'll never forget the level of faith you had in the books we did together over the years.

We also dedicate this book to our children, Nkem and Amara, who are glad we are done with *Mad Cash* and all the craziness that came with the territory.

Thanks to Michelle Howry, our new editor at Perigee, who had to hit the ground running from day one.

Emmanuel Modu & Andrea Walker

Contents

Part III: Taking Stock

Part IV: Having Some Funds

Part V: Money for Reading, 'Riting, and 'Rithmetic

Part VI: Looking into the Future

Introduction

For most young people, the biggest obstacle to investing is the amount of money they think is required to become investors. We wrote *Mad Cash: A First Timer's Guide to Investing $30 to $3,000* to show you how to safely invest your money no matter how modest the sum. In this book, we will introduce you to basic investment concepts and tell you what steps to take in order to build a nest egg for your future.

WHY SHOULD YOU READ THIS BOOK?

This book is an extension of our previous book, *Teen Vestor: The Practical Investment Guide for Teens and Their Parents*. That book was written primarily for teen investors or *Teenvestors*, as we call you, and its purpose was to teach young people about investment basics. *Mad Cash* is also written for Teenvestors, but it also provides you with step-by-step instructions on how to make your first investment with little money.

Why a special book for young investors? Because investors who are minors (less than 18 years of age in most states) have some special needs when it comes to investing. For example, you can't invest on your own without adult supervision. You may find it hard to open up and maintain regular bank accounts. And most of you can only make investments that require very little money, because you don't have lots of cash at your disposal.

USING YOUR BEST INVESTMENT ALLY—TIME

The most important thing is to get started right away because, when it comes to investing, time is your best friend. The sooner you begin, no matter how little money you have, the better your chances of growing your investment portfolio. The element of time gives you an advantage mainly because of the power of *compounding*, the phenomenon of how interest on your money helps your portfolio multiply in value over time. Compounding is described in detail in Chapter 2.

WHAT'S IN THIS BOOK?
Investment Categories

Mad Cash is in six parts:

- *Part I: Ready, Set, Invest*—Investment goals, the importance of compounding, and understanding investment risks

- *Part II: Stashing Your Cash*—Savings accounts, checking accounts, money market accounts, Certificates of Deposit, accounts in banks and credit unions

- *Part III: Taking Stock*—Stocks and direct investment plans

- *Part IV: Having Some Funds*—Mutual funds and exchange traded funds

- *Part V: Money for Readin', 'Riting, and 'Rithmetic*—College savings plans and Coverdell Educational Savings Accounts

- *Part VI: Looking into the Future*—Roth IRAs and U.S. Savings Bonds

With the exception of Parts I and II, which discuss investment basics and bank accounts, each investment product explained in this book generally has two sections: the basics of the investment product and the step-by-step process for investing in that product. With these instructions, you should have all the information you need to make your first investments.

Recommended Investment Amounts

While a Teenvestor can put even as little as $1 in some investments, such as stocks and direct investments, it doesn't make sense to invest such small amounts since you would be charged big brokerage fees relative to the sum you are investing. For example, at the time of this writing, a share of Lucent Technology stock is $1.50, so you can buy ten shares of Lucent Technology stock for a total of about $15 ($1.50 × 10 = $15). If it costs $10 in fees to make the purchase from a stockbroker, you would have to pay the broker $25 ($15 + $10 = $25) to buy ten shares of the stock. This means that the average cost per share, including the transaction fees, would be $2.50 ($25/10 shares = $2.50). On the other hand, if you purchased 200 shares of the stock for $300 (200 × $1.50 = $300) from the stockbroker, the transaction cost would still be $10, so you'd have to give the broker $310 dollars. This translates to an average cost per share, after considering fees, of $1.55 ($310/200 shares = $1.55).

As you can see, the more shares you buy, the lower your total cost per share. This phenomenon is true with lots of other investments for which you are charged fees and other transaction costs, besides stocks. In addition, some investments such as mutual funds (Chapter 12) have minimum required amounts that have nothing to do with transaction fees. For example, a popular mutual fund, the Vanguard 500 index, requires that you invest at least $1,000.

To help you avoid huge transaction costs, most investments in this book have a *recommended minimum investment* amount. In addition, each major investment category has a *minimum optional additional investment* amount. As an example, an investment called a direct investment plan (Chapter 10) requires an initial investment of about $300 to $500, depending on the company offering the plan. After the initial investment, you can add as little as $30 to $100 to make additional investments, depending on the company offering the plan.

At the beginning of most major investment categories, you will see a box similar to the one shown below, which clearly shows the recommended investments amount.

Direct Investment Plans

⇒ Recommended Minimum Investment $300 to $500
⇒ Minimum Additional Investment $30 to $100

The dollar amounts in both the recommended minimum investments and the minimum additional investments fall in the ranges listed in the box below. This will help you determine which investments you can afford to make right away, and which ones you should hold off on until you accumulate more money.

> **Investment Ranges for the Recommended Minimum Investment and Minimum Additional Investment (Optional)**
>
> | | | |
> |---|---|---|
> | $ | ⇒ | $30 to $100 |
> | $$ | ⇒ | $100 to $300 |
> | $$$ | ⇒ | $300 to $500 |
> | $$$$ | ⇒ | $500 to $1,000 |
> | $$$$$ | ⇒ | $1,000 to $3,000 |

Internet Resources

One of the great things about the Internet is that investment information is so readily available. This is both a blessing and a curse, so many investment-related websites can overwhelm a beginner. In *Mad Cash* we provide you with a list of the best investing websites to help you in your journey as a new investor. In addition, check out our website, www.teenvestor.com, where you can get updated information and more details about the topics discussed in the book. While Teenvestors make up 70% of our website's visitors, adults (especially parents) make up the remaining 30%.

WHO WE ARE

As mentioned earlier, we are the authors of the *TeenVestor: The Practical Investment Guide for Teens and Their Parents*. Together, both of us have spent the past 12 years writing about young people in business and teaching young people about investing and entrepreneurship. For several years, we ran a not-for-profit business camp, called Teen Business Camp, on the campuses of Rutgers University and The New Jersey Institute of Technology.

Emmanuel Modu honed his investing skills at Merrill Lynch as a senior treasury analyst, at J.P. Morgan Chase as a vice president, and at Citibank as a vice president. He attended University of Pennsylvania's Wharton School after receiving his undergraduate degree from Princeton University.

He is also the author of *The Lemonade Stand: A Guide to Encouraging the Entrepreneur in Your Child.*

Andrea Walker graduated from Princeton University, the George Washington School of Law, and Seton Hall Law School, where she received her master's in law.

We are married to each other and we are raising our children to become Teenvestors.

We have appeared on many television programs, including CNBC's "The Edge" and CNN Money, in many publications, including the *New York Daily News*, the *Wall Street Journal*, *Kiplinger's*, and *Forbes*, and on many websites, including Morningstar.com, Money.com, BusinessWeek Online, and others.

These days, we spend a lot more time communicating with young people through our website, www.teenvestor.com—the most comprehensive website for young investors. Whether on the Internet or in a classroom setting, we've discovered that young people have the capacity to learn about investing and entrepreneurship. More important, we've found ways to make business concepts fun and interesting. This book applies the techniques we've learned over the years to turn you into a successful Teenvestor.

PART

1

Ready, Set, Invest

1

Scoring Some Goals

Goals are wants, needs, and future objectives that you set for yourself. Because this is a financial book, we will only discuss financial goals. The first step to successful investing is setting your financial goals.

Are you investing to save for a major purchase in the future, such as a new car, a college education, or a computer? The answer to this question is very important because it will, most likely, influence your investment strategy. For example, if the major expenditures you are saving for are far off in the future, you may feel comfortable taking on a little more risk than if those expenditures are just around the bend. Your portfolio may have more stocks in it than it would if you are investing to satisfy short-term needs. This is because the farther in the future you need the money, the less you will have to worry about the temporary ups and downs of the financial markets. By contrast, if you expect to make a large expenditure in the next two or three months, you may be better off putting your money in a bank investment product, like a Certificate of Deposit, a money market account, or even just an ordinary bank account. So you can see that the farther away your expenditure, the more risk you can afford to take.

LISTING YOUR GOALS

Make a list of your financial goals. Trust us—the simple act of putting your goals down on paper helps you focus on the things that are important to you. Next, decide how many months or years you have to meet each specific goal, because when you invest, you'll need to find an investment option that fits your time frame for accomplishing your goals. Knowing how much time you have to meet your goals will help you decide how much risk you can take on. Classify your goals in the following time categories:

- *Short-term:* Goals to be accomplished within a year
- *Medium-term:* Goals to be accomplished between two and four years
- *Long-term:* Goals to be accomplished in five years or more

If you ask your parents what type of time periods they attach to short-term, medium-term, and long-term goals, you will probably find that their time periods are longer than those shown above. For many adults, short-term, medium-term, and long-term translate to time frames of one year, five years, and ten years or more. You, on the other hand, have much shorter time frames for these categories simply because you have not lived as long. A year may seem like an eternity to you! But in the life of your money, it's not long at all.

Your success as a Teenvestor will depend on your ability to think farther into the future than your peers. While we know that it would be too much to ask you to think 20 years into the future, the longer your time horizon for your goals, the better your chances of reaching them. The rea-

---

BOX 1.1
My Goals

Financial Goals	Time to Reach Your Goals
_____	_____
_____	_____
_____	_____
_____	_____
_____	_____
_____	_____
_____	_____
_____	_____
_____	_____
_____	_____
_____	_____

---

son for this is simple—time is the best friend of all investors, and Teenvestors have plenty of it compared to old investors.

Teenvestors generally include college, cars, computers, games, and cash savings amounts as some of their goals. Box 1.1 is a template for listing your financial goals, and Box 1.2 is an example of a Teenvestor's financial goals.

Notice that in Box 1.2, you'll find examples of short-term, medium-term, and long-term goals. If your goal is to become a millionaire, you will probably have to put that as a long-term goal. Unless you happen to win a lottery or you inherit great wealth from a relative, this is going to take a while. On the other hand, buying $200 worth of Microsoft stock is something that you may be able to do in a few months by saving $50 per month, for example, or by applying cash gifts from relatives to the purchase.

MEETING YOUR GOALS

After listing your goals, you should then establish a plan on how to meet these goals. First, prioritize which goals are most important to you, and

BOX 1.2
Example: Teenvestor Goals

Saving/Investment/Life Goals	Time to Reach Your Goal
Buying $200 of Microsoft Stock	5 Months (short-term)
Going to College	3 Years (medium-term)
Having $100,000 by Age 33	20 Years (long-term)
Buying a Car	5 Years (long-term)
Buying a Computer Game with	
Holiday Cash Gift from Relatives	6 Months (short-term)

then make a plan on how to get the money to save for the expenditure. Most investment experts will tell you that unless you make a real effort to put money aside for investing, you will never be a steady investor. A phrase you will hear time and time again is "pay yourself first." This is another way of saying that you should be in the habit of saving a portion of every penny that goes into your hands for the purpose of investing it.

In order to set aside this money, you have to keep track of what money flows through your hands. One easy way to do this is to create a monthly budget. It doesn't matter if you get $1 per month or $200 per month from your sources of cash. What matters is that creating a monthly budget is a habit that will help you become a good saver and investor in the long run, and that will help you meet your financial goals.

Most Teenvestors don't have a steady source of income besides their allowance, part-time jobs, extra chores around the house, and occasional cash

BOX 1.4
Websites to Help You Manage Your Finances

Securities & Exchange Commission
www.sec.gov

American Savings Education Council
www.asec.org

Federal Consumer Information Center
www.pueblo.gsa.gov

Treasury Direct
www.publicdebt.treas.gov

The Investor's Clearinghouse
www.investoreducation.org

Federal Deposit Insurance
www.fdic.gov

BOX 1.3
Monthly Budget Worksheet

Sources of Cash

Money from parents (allowance, etc.)   _____
Cash gifts from relatives   _____
Money from jobs   _____
Money from your own business   _____
Total Sources of Cash   _____

Expenses

Amount You Pay Yourself   _____
Lunch   _____
Snacks/Food   _____
School Materials   _____
Clothing   _____
Magazine/Internet Subscriptions   _____
Transportation (buses, subway, etc.)   _____
Gas (if you drive)   _____
Oil (if you drive)   _____
Other Expenses   _____
Total Expenses   _____

Total Sources of Cash Minus Total Expenses   _____

gifts from relatives. We recommend that if you receive an allowance from your parents, you keep a portion aside to invest. We have interacted with a lot of Teenvestors, and we see this time and time again—when parents realize that you are allocating money for investment purposes or that you are creating a budget, they are more likely to increase your allowance accordingly. Our first book, *TeenVestor: The Practical Investment Guide for Teens and Their Parents*, goes into more details of the sources of cash for Teenvestors. There are also many books on how to do your own personal financial planning, which will help you save money for the purposes of investing over a long period of time.

2

Money Multiplication through Compounding

When it comes to investing, time is your biggest ally. The combination of time and the principle of *compounding* play a major role in helping investors meet their investment goals. Compounding is such an important concept that we have devoted this entire chapter to it.

With compounding, interest or "returns" are paid on previously earned interest, as well as on your original deposit or investment. Compounding is what can make it possible for your investments to really grow. Remember the goal stated by a Teenvestor in Box 1.2 in Chapter 1—to have $100,000 by the time he is 33? Through the power of compounding, a Teenvestor who can invest about $130 per month in an investment that earns a 10% yearly compounded interest over a 20-year period can indeed see his investments grow to $100,000.

Your money multiplies much faster with compounding than without it. The significance of this statement will sink in with a real example. Let's look at a bank account to see how the principle of compounding works.

In the banking world, when you deposit your money in a bank, you are in effect lending money to that bank. In return, your bank may promise to pay you interest. *Interest* is the fee a borrower pays to a lender for the use of the borrowed money.

Banks can either promise you *simple interest* or *compound interest*. If a bank pays simple interest on your deposit, it will only pay you interest based on the original amount that you deposit into the account. By contrast, if a bank pays compound interest, it will pay you interest on the interest that you accumulate on your deposit, which we refer to as *interest-on-interest*. The bottom line, as you will discover later in this chapter, is that compounding of interest means a lot more money for you.

STEP-BY-STEP EXAMPLE OF COMPOUNDING

To fully understand compounding, you must appreciate what it means *not* to compound interest. Remember that when interest is not compounded, it is called simple interest. Here now are examples of simple and compound interest.

Simple Interest

Suppose a bank promises you 10% simple interest on your deposit of $1,000. At the end of the first year, after you've made the deposit, you would receive $100 in interest ($1,000 × 10% = $100), thereby increasing your original investment of $1,000 to $1,100.

During the second year, the bank again pays you $100 in interest, which is calculated again as 10% of your original investment of $1,000 ($1,000 × 10% =

BOX 2.1
Total Value of a $1,000 One-Time Deposit
(Simple Interest)

Years Elapsed	At 10% Simple Interest
1	$1,100
2	$1,200
7	$1,700
10	$2,000
20	$3,000
40	$5,000
50	$6,000

$100). At the end of the second year, your original investment has grown from $1,000 to $1,200, or by $100 each year.

Box 2.1 shows the value of a one-time deposit into an account earning simple interest at the rate of 10% per year.

Compound Interest

Suppose the same bank now promises you 10% interest compounded annually on your deposit of $1,000. At the end of the first year in which you made your $1,000 deposit, you would receive $100 in interest ($1,000 × 10% = $100), increasing your original investment of $1,000 to $1,100. This is the same as with the simple interest example above, but watch what happens next.

At the end of the second year, you will be paid interest based on an investment of $1,100, which is a combination of your original investment of $1,000 plus the interest that was paid in the first year of $100. That means you will receive $110 ($1,100 × 10% = $110) in the second year. Your investment now grows to $1,210 ($1,100 + $110 = $1,210) with compound interest as opposed to $1,200 with simple interest.

BOX 2.2
Total Value of a $1,000 One-Time Deposit
(Compound Interest)

Years Elapsed	At 10% Compound Interest
1	$1,100
2	$1,210
7	$1,949
10	$2,594
20	$6,728
40	$45,259
50	$117,391

The Advantage of Compounding Over Time

Our examples above showed that a $1,000 deposit earning 10% yearly interest had a total value over a one-year period of $1,100 for both simple and compound interest. Over a two-year period, however, the total value of the deposit for simple and compound interest are $1,200 and $1,210 respectively. Box 2.3 below shows the difference between compound and simple interest offered by a bank over a one-year, two-year, seven-year, ten-

BOX 2.3
Total Value of a $1,000 One-Time Deposit

Years Elapsed	At 10% Simple Interest	At 10% Compound Interest	Difference*
1	$1,100	$1,100	$0
2	$1,200	$1,210	$10
7	$1,700	$1,949	$249
10	$2,000	$2,594	$594
20	$3,000	$6,728	$3,728
40	$5,000	$45,259	$40,259
50	$6,000	$117,391	$111,391

*Total value at compound interest minus total at simple interest

year, 20-year, 40-year, and 50-year period. As you can see, over time, the benefits of compounding become more and more dramatic.

THE RULE OF 72

The *Rule of 72* is a formula used to quickly calculate approximately how much time it will take you to double your investment given any compound interest rate. The Rule of 72 formula is as follows:

72 / (Compound Interest Rate) = Years to Double Your Money

To apply this to our earlier example in Box 2.3, here is how to calculate how much time it will take you to double your initial investment of $1,000 in a bank account earning 10% compound interest:

72 / 10 = 7.2 years

Note that in Box 2.3, the compound interest column shows a balance of $1,949 in year seven at a 10% compound rate. This is close to twice the initial investment of $1,000, so the Rule of 72 formula works.

The power of compounding applies to more than just bank deposits. It applies to *all* investments, especially investments in the stock market. While you don't earn interest if you buy a share of stock, investment experts have calculated that the type of average ***return***—the amount that the value of your stock will go up—you can expect to earn in the stocks of very large companies is a compound interest rate of approximately 10% per year over a long period of time. This is based on an analysis of the gains in the stock market over a 70-year period and on the assumption that you will reinvest back into stocks all the money you earn in ***dividends,*** defined as profits paid out to stockholders by the company.

Once again, this 10% compound return in the stock market can only be achieved if you keep your money in the market for a long period of time; in other words, if you are a long-term investor. If you are investing in stocks, your investment strategy should include making sure that you put your money back into your investments by purchasing additional shares of stock to ensure that you receive the benefits of compounding. Over time, you will find that this makes a huge difference in the amount that you earn.

Know the Downside

Risk can generally be described as the possibility that your investments will go up or down in value. Money has its own way of rewarding or punishing investors for taking risks. As a rule of thumb, you should expect that the riskier your investment, the greater your potential gains or losses. Understanding investments in terms of risk is an important step in learning how to be a smart and savvy investor. In this chapter, we discuss related risks that you will face as a Teenvestor such as credit risk, market risk, and fraud risk.

CREDIT RISK

Credit risk generally refers to the risk that the company in which you have invested will go bankrupt. It is easier to describe this type of risk by looking at *bonds*, loans given to corporations or even governments. When you buy a

BOX 3.1
Risks and Rewards

As a rule of thumb, you should expect that the more investment risk you take, the more you should expect to get rewarded or punished for your actions.

U.S. Savings Bond, you are giving a loan to the U.S. government, and when you buy a corporate bond, such as a General Electric bond, you are giving a loan to the corporation. Of course, the U.S. government and the corporation will pay you interest on these bonds. If you buy a U.S. Savings Bond, the interest you will receive on the bond will generally be less than the interest you would be paid if you bought a General Electric bond. This difference exists because the government *guarantees* a U.S. Savings Bond, and there is very little likelihood that the government will renege on paying its debts. All the government has to do, if it is having problems paying its debts, is to increase taxes.

On the other hand, if a corporation like General Electric has major problems paying its debt, it can simply stop paying interest, declare bankruptcy, and, if possible, negotiate with lenders on how to pay back its loans. Since you take on more risk by lending to corporations than by lending to the federal government, you should expect higher rewards in the form of interest rates with corporate investments than with government investments. This higher interest rate reflects the credit risk of the corporate bond—that is, the risk that General Electric will not pay you back the money it owes you.

How do you know the credit risk of a company? *Rating agencies* such as Standard Poor's and Moody's Investors

BOX 3.2
Top Ten U.S. Bankruptcies*
(Pre-Bankruptcy Assets in Parenthesis)

#1 WorldCom, Inc. in 2002 ($103.9 billion)

#2 Enron in 2001 ($63.4 billion)

#3 Conseco, Inc. in 2002 ($52.2 billion)

#4 Texaco in 1987 ($35.9 billion)

#5 Financial Corp. of America in 1988 ($33.9 billion)

#6 Global Crossing in 2002 ($25.5 billion)

#7 UAL Corporation in 2002 ($25.2 billion)

#8 Adelphi Communications in 2002 ($24.4 billion)

#9 Pacific Gas & Electric Co. in 2001 ($21.5 billion)

#10 MCORP in 1989 ($20.2 billion)

*Bankruptcy list as of 1/6/03

BOX 3.3
Return and Interest

A *return* is the amount of money you make on an investment, and it is expressed as a percentage of your initial investment. You can think of *interest* as the return on the money you lend to a bank (such as your bank deposits) or to corporations (such as when you buy a corporate bond). Return is a broad term for how much money you earn on an investment since not all investments earn interest.

For example, stocks don't earn interest, so the return on stocks will be calculated based on the profit you can make on the investment if you sold it. To be more specific suppose you buy General Electric stock for $25 and it goes to $30 one year later, your return is calculated as follows:

(Ending Value − Beginning Value) / Beginning Value = Return ($30 − $25)/$25 = 20%

Services, have rating systems that tell you the relative credit risk of each major company. For more information on credit risks, see the following websites:

- www.standardandpoors.com
- www.moodys.com

MARKET RISK

Market risk is the risk that the value of your investment (usually stock investments for our purposes) will go down due to a general downturn in the economy. A bad economy decreases the amount of money most companies make and the value of a company's stock. The reason is that consumers—people like you and us who buy goods and services from companies—drive the economy. If the economy is in bad shape, some consumers lose their jobs and some will save their money because they are scared of getting laid off. This, of course, affects the amount of money consumers spend, and affects the profits companies make. As a Teenvestor, you will discover that company profits are a major part of what drives stock prices of companies.

Besides hearing about a bad economy in the news, one of the ways you can tell if the economy is doing poorly is to watch the decrease in a stock market index, such as the S&P 500. You will learn more about this index and other indices in Chapter 8. From 2000 to 2002, this index did something that it hadn't done since the years 1939 to 1941: it went down in value for three consecutive years. Specifically, it went down in value in 2000 by 10%, in 2001 by 13%, and in 2002 by 23%. Such decreases tell you that investors during those years faced great market risks.

There are other ways to tell if investors are facing market risks, too. Has the number of people who have lost their jobs increased? Has the amount of interest businesses are paying to borrow money increased? These market risk indicators are beyond the scope of this book, but they are fully described in our book, *TeenVestor: The Practical Investment Guide for Teens and Their Parents*, and in other investment guides.

Knowing that you face market risk means that you will have to be careful about the type of companies or products in which you invest. The lessons most investors have learned in a bad market are that you should:

1. Never put all your money in one type of investment, such as stocks.

2. Never let anyone, including those glamorous Wall Street analysts on television, convince you that the value of investments *always* goes up (as stock values generally did from 1991 to 1999).

3. Always research companies on your own to see if they are good investment candidates.

4. Always look for "good buys," strong companies whose stock prices are a little down but will most likely rebound given their track record.

BOX 3.4
Wayward Teenvestors Run Afoul of the Law

To be sure, scam artists are in all areas of business, but we found the charges against two wayward Teenvestors to be particularly interesting because of their youth, their use of the Internet, and, as you will read below, the simplicity of their alleged schemes.

In 2000, 15-year-old Jonathan Lebed became the youngest person ever charged with violating Securities and Exchange Commission (SEC) regulations. It is illegal to knowingly make false statements about the value of a security. Jonathan was accused of doing just that by falsely promoting, through Internet chat groups and message boards, stocks of a handful of small companies (also known as "penny stocks" or "micro-cap stocks"). The SEC alleged that Jonathan was involved in what is known as a classic "pump-and-dump" scheme whereby the promoter of a stock is dumping (selling) his stash of stocks while touting its virtues. Jonathan settled the case with the SEC without admitting or denying guilt and he gave back nearly $300,000 of the $800,000 he made in the transactions that were challenged by the SEC.

Another Teenvestor who had a run-in with the SEC was 17-year-old Cole Bartiromo. In 2002, Cole was charged with running a phony million-dollar online investment scam. Those who were scammed by Cole should have known something was rotten when Cole allegedly offered an investment with a one-week 250% risk-free return. It gets even better! Apparently, he allegedly also offered investors a "Christmas miracle" investment option in which these "lucky" individuals would earn a 2,500% return. In addition to turning $900,000 over to the SEC (which he allegedly hid away in a Costa Rican casino account), Cole had to disclose full details of his operation. For what it's worth, Cole settled the case with the SEC without admitting to or denying the allegations against him.

The bottom line is that you should never 1) invest in penny or micro-cap stocks, 2) get investment advice from an Internet chat room or message board, and 3) believe in excessive returns!

BOX 3.5
Red Flag Phrases

In the world of investing, there are certain words or phrases that should make you proceed with caution.

Watch out when you hear potential investments characterized in the following terms:

- Guaranteed return on your stock
- Miracle stock
- A sure win, or sure bet
- It's too complicated to explain
- Hurry, invest now—it won't be around much longer
- Quick profit in a short time
- Multi-level marketing
- Everyone is investing in it
- Penny stocks

FRAUD

Fraud has become something that investors always have to beware of. Most recently, some high-profile bankruptcies such as Enron and World-Com were triggered by fraud and other chicanery. We will discuss this type of fraud later on in this section, but the typical types of fraud Teenvestors will run into are of the less elaborate kind that are easily avoidable. They are well chronicled by the *Securities and Exchange Commission* or *SEC*, the U.S. government agency that regulates the investment community. Box 3.4 shows some simple frauds perpetrated by wayward Teenvestors, according to the Securities and Exchange Commission.

Easily Avoidable Fraud

We've seen investment offers that promise to pay sky-high interest rates for what are, at best, extremely risky propositions—and at worst, pure frauds. Here is a list of red flags that the Securities & Exchange Commission says should make investors suspicious of an investment offer:

- *It sounds too good to be true.* Mom was right! Compare promised returns or interest rates with returns on a well-known stock index such as The Dow Jones Industrial Average and a bond benchmark such as U.S. Savings Bonds (both of which you will learn about in subsequent chapters). Any investment that promises you substantially more than these readily available indexes is, by definition risky. Risk is not necessarily a bad thing, because with more risk there is the potential that you can make more money. However, you should know how risky something is before investing in it.

- *An unusually high "guaranteed return."* Most fraudsters spend a lot of time trying to convince investors that their investments offer extremely high returns, which are "guaranteed." If a person or a company that is not well known tells you that an unusually high return is "guaranteed," watch out!! Even if you know the company, if your guaranteed profit sounds too high, you may not be aware of all the risk involved.

- *A company that is not well known.* If you've never heard of a company, broker, or adviser, spend some time checking them out before you make your investment. Most public companies make electronic filings with the Securities and Exchange Commission, or (www.sec.gov), and computer databases exist to help you research brokers and advisers. Your state securities regulator may have additional information. Incidentally, if a supposedly upright financial firm lists only a post office box as an address, you'll want to do a lot of work before sending it your money. And if anyone mentions the words *penny stocks*—stocks that trade for less than $1—run away as fast as you can.

• *Being pressured to invest "right now."* Scam artists usually try to create a sense of urgency, making you think that if you don't act *now*, you'll miss out on a fabulous opportunity. But savvy Teenvestors take time to do their homework before investing. If you're being pressured to invest, especially if it is a "once-in-a-lifetime," "too-good-to-be-true" opportunity that you "just can't miss," just say no. Your wallet will thank you.

• *An investment that is hard to understand.* Con artists frequently use a lot of big words and technical-sounding phrases to impress you. But have faith in yourself! If you don't understand an investment, don't buy it. If a salesman isn't able to explain a concept clearly enough for you to understand, it isn't your fault. Don't make it your problem by investing in the product. Lest you think that fraud only happens to beginning or inexperienced investors, Wall Street experts have also been victims, as evidenced by the WorldCom and Enron bankruptcies, the largest two bankruptcies in U.S. history. See Appendix I for an explanation of the role fraud played in these bankruptcies.

Fraud That Is More Difficult to Avoid

The type of fraud that is more difficult to protect yourself against is the fraud perpetrated by some big corporations. There were so many corporate fraud cases in 2002 that we have been flooded with questions on our website from Teenvestors who ask, "Who can we trust?" We tell them that the U.S. stock market is the biggest and most well-respected market in the world and that the government and business people are putting controls in place to make sure the market is fair for all investors. The sections below describe prominent corporate fraud cases and what the government is doing to take corruption out of the financial markets.

Corporate Shenanigans

Earlier, when we discussed the concept of risks and rewards, we told you that if an investment sounds too good to be true, it is probably a scam. Most of the time people can spot a scam when they see one. But what do you do when companies or rogue investment analysts from reputable firms purposely deceive you about the condition of a company? In 2002, corporate dishonesty came to a head, and was part of the reason the stock market took a serious dive as investors lost confidence in the financial statements of many American companies. A long list of companies like Enron, WorldCom, Tyco, Merrill Lynch, Xerox, Merck, and Arthur Andersen had serious credibility issues about the truthfulness of their financial statements or their business ethics. WorldCom, for example, appears to have deliberately fabricated $9 billion worth of sales practically out of thin air.

At the time of this writing, the President and Congress were working on steps to restore confidence in the financial markets. There will probably be stiffer penalties for companies that tamper with their financial statements to deceive the public, and there may be other restrictions imposed on the reporting of executive compensation in the future. It's too early to tell what legislation will be put in place to stop the rigging of financial statements, but the public is mad and taking their anger out on the stock market. Given the importance of the U.S. stock market to the global economy, the government has made it a priority to take steps to restore confidence in the U.S. financial markets.

While we can't yet report on the progress being made to stop the big scandals related to financial statements, we can, however, report on the progress made by the Attorney General of New York in ensuring that investment bank analysts give honest information about companies to the public. An explanation of this will help you understand why it's important to do your own investment research and not to depend solely on so-called experts to tell you which investments you should make.

The Problem with Analysts and the Landmark Settlement by Investment Banks and the Attorney General of New York

During the go-go days of the Internet, a rogue Merrill Lynch analyst allegedly told unsuspecting investors that the stock of InfoSpace, a technology company whose stock is now worth about $9 per share after having reached a high of $130 per share, was a good buy. Unbeknown to these investors, the analyst who recommended the stock knew otherwise; in an internal email, he had declared that InfoSpace was "a piece of junk."

Unfortunately, as illustrated in the above example, a problem with some analysts in investment banks is that they are not as impartial as you would expect them to be when giving their opinions about stocks and other investments. Because they get business from the company whose stock they are pushing, they have an incentive to make the company look good. Fortunately for investors, a group led by New York Attorney General Eliot Spitzer reached two landmark agreements with Merrill Lynch and with a group of prominent investment firms. These agreements will probably set the standard for how brokerage firms will do business in the future. First, a fine was imposed on Merrill Lynch. The company also agreed to the following conditions:

- If an investment bank gives an opinion about any company, it must disclose any business arrangement it has with that company;
- Analysts' salaries are no longer tied to investment banking fees;
- Managers on the investment banking side will have no say as to how much analysts get paid; and
- Emails between analysts and investment bankers will be monitored to look for conflicts of interest.

In addition, a group of brokerage firms that includes Citigroup, Credit Suisse First Boston, Solomon Smith Barney, Deutsche Bank, Goldman Sachs, J.P. Morgan Chase, Lehman Brothers, Morgan Stanley, and UBS

Warburg collectively agreed to pay $1.4 billion to settle charges of biased and misleading research. In addition, they agreed to change the way they do business in order to restore the confidence in the financial markets.

While the agreement reached with investment banks will not resolve all the conflict of interest issues in investment firms, it is a good start at protecting the interests of investors that use the services of investment firms.

PART
2

Stashing Your Cash

4

Plain-Vanilla Savings

The first step for any young person who wants to become a Teenvestor is to establish a bank account. Without an account, you probably won't be able to accumulate enough money for investing because you will be tempted to dip into your on-hand cash from time to time. In addition, bank accounts make it easier for you to buy stocks, mutual funds, and other investment assets without having to send a check or money order to make the purchases.

You can open one or more of the following types of bank accounts:

- Savings account
- Checking account
- Money market account
- Certificate of Deposit (CD)

In this chapter, we will discuss savings and checking accounts, and the safety of your money in banks. Other bank products, such as money market accounts and Certificates of Deposit, are discussed in subsequent chapters.

A SAVINGS ACCOUNT
Why Start a Savings Account?

• *It is good for stashing small amounts.* A savings account is a good place to put small amounts of money that you will need in a short period of time.

• *It is a good place to start investing.*

As an investment vehicle, a savings account is not the best choice that you can make because the interest you earn on it can be miniscule—sometimes around 1%. However, a savings account is not a bad start if you have very little money. You can use this account to save enough money to invest in stocks and bonds at a later date.

General Types of Savings Accounts

• *Passbook savings account.* With a passbook savings account, you receive a record book in which your deposits and withdrawals are recorded to keep track of transactions on your account. This record book must be presented when you make deposits and withdrawals.

• *Statement savings account.* With a statement savings account, the bank regularly mails you a statement that shows your withdrawals and deposits for your account. Banks may charge a fee, such as a minimum balance fee, on statement savings accounts, if the balance falls below a specified sum.

BOX 4.1
Custodial Accounts

Custodial accounts are accounts for minors (generally those less than 18 years old). Custodial accounts are necessary because minors are not allowed to enter into any financial transactions (such as opening bank accounts or stock trading accounts). The adult who opens the account for a minor is considered the custodian of the account, but technically the assets in the account belong to the minor and are listed in the minor's name. The minor, however, cannot take control of the assets until he reaches majority age, which is generally 18 in most states.

Parents, grandparents, and other relatives frequently open up custodial accounts for related minors. As custodians, they are responsible for managing the account and making all important decisions about the account. Examples of custodial accounts are custodial savings accounts (in banks) and custodial brokerage accounts (for buying and selling stock through brokers). While the custodian controls the account, there is nothing to prohibit minors who know how to handle money from making suggestions about investments, such as stock purchases, which would be made through brokerage custodial accounts.

While the biggest advantage of custodial accounts is that they allow minors to save money in the banks and to buy and sell stock in custodial brokerage accounts, they also have other advantages. Some banks have lower balance requirements and lower fees for custodial savings accounts. In addition, taxes are lower on the profits minors make on their custodial brokerage accounts.

Teenvestors and Custodial Accounts

Minors (generally those less than 18 years old) can't open a bank account or other financial account on their own. Instead, an adult must open a *custodial account* for you. (See Box 4.1.) The adult, known as the *custodian*, is legally responsible for the account, but the account is established to benefit you.

Also, you are the legal owner of everything in the account. Upon reaching 18 (21 in some states), you will assume full responsibility for the account.

As we will discuss in later chapters, custodial accounts are necessary in order for you to purchase stocks and mutual funds from online brokers.

Accounts can be set up through banks or through brokers for Teenvestors' investment activities.

What Makes Opening Accounts So Expensive?

If you don't already have a bank account, you may be surprised at the fees banks charge. Nearly all banks impose fees on accounts, and these fees vary from bank to bank. Fortunately, fees on custodial accounts for minors are typically less than fees for regular accounts. In some cases, banks waive fees on custodial accounts altogether.

Some institutions charge a maintenance or flat monthly fee (such as $15 per month) regardless of how much money you keep in your account. Others charge a fee if the minimum balance in your account drops below a certain amount (such as $1,500, for example). It's important to learn what fees your bank charges and to look for a bank with the lowest fees. See Chapter 7 for more information on picking the right account.

For example, suppose you can only afford to put $150 in your savings account and a bank charges you a monthly account maintenance fee of $15 a month for balances under $1,500. Your bank account, then, will go down to $135 in the first month after you open the account, to $120 in the second month, and so on. By the tenth month after opening your account, your initial $150 savings would be reduced to zero due to the $15 per month fee.

CHECKING ACCOUNT

With a checking account, you use checks to withdraw money from the account. You can usually make as many deposits into the account as you wish. Many institutions will enable you to withdraw from or deposit funds to a checking account through an automated teller machine (ATM) or to pay for purchases at stores with your ATM card by deducting money from your automated teller account.

BOX 4.2
FDIC Insurance

The Federal Deposit Insurance Corporation (FDIC) is an independent agency of the U.S. government that was established in 1933 to insure bank deposits. FDIC-insured deposits are backed by the full faith and credit of the United States.

All types of deposits received by a financial institution are insured. For example, savings deposits, checking deposits, Christmas Club accounts, and Certificates of Deposits (CDs) are all insured deposits. Stocks, bonds, mutual funds, and other investments, however, are not covered by deposit insurance.

The $100,000 insurance limit is for each bank (not each branch of the bank) in which you have your money. So, for example, if you have money in two different branches of Fleet Bank, you can recover no more than $100,000 of your money if the bank goes bankrupt. On the other hand, if you have money in Fleet Bank, Citibank, and Chase Manhattan Bank, you can recover a total of $100,000 from each bank, or $300,000.

Varieties of Checking Accounts

Different banks call their checking accounts by different names, but there are two basic types of checking accounts offered by all banks:

- *Regular checking account.* Sometimes called a "demand deposit account." This account does not pay interest.

- *Negotiable Order of Withdrawal (NOW) account.* This account pays interest.

The typical adult investor probably has a checking account. We don't, however, recommend checking accounts for Teenvestors because of the hefty fees some banks charge. Checking account fees are typically higher than fees for savings accounts, and the minimum required balances (in order to avoid these fees) are higher as well. If you would like the convenience of a checking account, perhaps you can strike a deal with your parents so that you can keep your money in their checking accounts and have them write checks on your behalf when you need checks.

HOW SAFE ARE BANKS?

A phrase you'll hear when you begin looking into bank accounts is *FDIC insured*. Here are some things you need to know about this type of insurance:

- *FDIC*. FDIC stands for Federal Deposit Insurance Corporation. The FDIC insurance was created by the federal government to insure the deposits you make in a bank. Only deposit accounts at federally insured depository institutions are protected by FDIC insurance.

- *$100,000 of protection*. The insurance protects the money you have on deposit to a limit of $100,000. So if your bank goes bankrupt, your deposits less than or equal to $100,000 are safe. Any deposits more than $100,000 are not protected by FDIC insurance. (See Box 4.2 for more details on FDIC insurance.)

- *Not all bank-offered products are covered*. Federally insured banks also offer products that are *not* protected by FDIC insurance. For example, many banks offer products like mutual funds (which we will discuss in a later chapter). Mutual funds are not covered by FDIC insurance, and thus are not protected by the federal government. If you are not sure whether the product offered by a bank is protected by FDIC insurance, just ask.

Bank CD and Money Market Deposit Accounts		
Money Market Deposit		
$$$$$ ⇒ Recommended Minimum Investment	$1,000 to $3,000
$$$$$ ⇒ Minimum Additional Investment (Optional)	$1,000 to $3,000
CDs		
$$$$ ⇒ Recommended Minimum Investment	$500 to $1,000
$$$$ ⇒ Minimum Additional Investment (Optional)	$500 to $1,000

5

Spicing Up Your Savings with CDs and Money Market Accounts

Savings and checking accounts are nothing special when you consider the amount of interest they pay. Once you have accumulated more cash, you should consider other bank products, such as money market deposit accounts and Certificates of Deposit.

MONEY MARKET DEPOSIT ACCOUNTS

Most banks offer an interest-bearing account that allows you to write checks, called a *money market deposit account* (MMDA). MMDAs are different from regular checking accounts in a few important ways:

- *It offers higher interest rates.* MMDAs pay a higher rate of interest than regular checking or savings accounts.

• *It requires higher minimum balance.* MMDAs require that you have on deposit a higher minimum balance than regular checking or savings accounts. Typically, these accounts pay an escalating amount of interest that depends on the balance you keep in the account. In other words, the higher the balance you keep in the account, the higher the interest the bank pays you.

• *It offers limited check-writing abilities.* While you are allowed to write checks on these accounts, you are limited in the number of checks that you may write (generally a handful of checks per month). As is the case with most accounts, there may be fees associated with maintaining an MMDA.

CERTIFICATE OF DEPOSIT

Checking, savings, or money market deposit accounts are great places to keep money you may need in the next few weeks or months. But if you don't need all your money right away, you may want to put some of it into a special kind of bank account called a *Certificate of Deposit (CD)* or *time deposit*. Here are some important things you need to know about a CD:

• *It offers a guaranteed interest rate for a period of time.* CDs usually offer a guaranteed rate of interest for a specified time period, such as six months or one year. The *term*—or time period of the investment—of the CD can range from several days to several years. Once you have chosen the term, the bank will generally require that you keep your money in the account until the term ends (for example, until maturity).

• *It offers higher rates than other bank deposits.* Because you agree to leave your funds in the account for a specified period of time, the institution will generally pay you a higher rate of interest than it would for a savings, checking, or money market deposit account.

BOX 5.1
Comparison of Various Bank Accounts

Type of Account	Will I Earn Interest?	May I Write Checks?	Are There Withdrawal Limitations?	Are There Any Fees/ Penalties on the Account?
Savings Account	Yes	No	Yes, a few transfers per month	Yes, fees for small balances
Regular Checking Account	No	Yes	No	Yes, fees for small balances
Interest Checking (NOW) Account	Yes	Yes	No	Yes, fees for small balances
Money Market Deposit Account (MMDA)	Yes, usually higher than a NOW or savings account	Yes, only three per month	Yes, a few transfers per month	Yes, fees for small balances
Certificate of Deposit (CD)	Yes, usually higher than a MMDA	No	Yes, usually no withdrawals are allowed until the date of maturity	Yes, if you withdraw principal funds before the date of maturity

• *It offers a notification of maturity.* Banks will notify you before the maturity date for most CDs. Often CDs renew automatically. Therefore, if you do not notify the institution at maturity that you wish to take out your money, the CD will roll over (continue) for another term.

• *It has a penalty for early withdrawal.* Sometimes a bank will allow you to withdraw your principal before maturity, but a penalty is frequently charged. Penalties vary among banks, and they can be heavy. In fact, the penalty could be greater than the amount of interest earned, so you could lose a part of your initial deposit.

Credit Union Savings, Checking, Share Certificates (CDs), and Money Market Deposit Accounts		
Savings Account		
$ ⇒	Recommended Minimum Investment	$30 to $100
$ ⇒	Minimum Additional Investment (Optional)	$30 to $100
Checking Account		
$$$$ ⇒	Recommended Minimum Investment	$500 to $1,000
⇒	Minimum Additional Investment (Optional)	None
Share Certificates (CDs)		
$$$$ ⇒	Recommended Minimum Investment	$500 to $1,000
$$$$ ⇒	Minimum Additional Investment (Optional)	$500 to $1,000
Money Market Deposit		
$$$$$ ⇒	Recommended Minimum Investment	$1,000 to $3,000
$$$$$ ⇒	Minimum Additional Investment (Optional)	$1,000 to $3,000

6

Credit Unions:
The Alternative to Banks

A *federal credit union* is a nonprofit financial institution owned and run by its members. Organized to serve, democratically controlled credit unions provide their members with a safe place to save and borrow at reasonable rates. The money the members deposit in the credit union is used to make loans to fellow credit union members.

WHAT IS A CREDIT UNION?

There are nearly 10,000 credit unions in the United States servicing more than 79 million people. In general, these institutions offer their members the following services and advantages:

- *The same products as banks*. Credit unions offer the same basic services and products offered by banks: savings accounts, checking accounts, Share Certificates (the credit union equivalent of CDs), money market deposit accounts, home loans, and automobile loans.

- *Competitive rates.* Credit unions offer rates on savings accounts, checking accounts, Share Certificates, auto loans, house loans, and credit card accounts that are competitive with those of banks. They also have more leeway in the rates they charge their customers because they are nonprofit.

- *Lower balances and fees.* In general, it's easier to avoid paying fees on credit union accounts because credit unions typically require lower minimum balances. They also charge lower fees to maintain accounts. From this point of view, credit unions are better for Teenvestors than regular banks.

- *Special accounts for young investors/savers.* Some credit unions have special accounts for Teenvestors and those young adults who are just starting out in their careers. For example, in the credit union we belong to, we have established custodial savings accounts for our children for which we pay no fees for small balances. In addition, our credit union offers free checking accounts for people from ages 18 to 29 and free ATM cards with no-fee withdrawals.

WHO CAN JOIN A CREDIT UNION?

To join a credit union, you must be eligible for membership. Each institution decides whom it will serve. Most credit unions are organized to serve people in a particular community, group or groups of employees, or members of an organization or association. If your parents are eligible to join a credit union, they can also get you an account at that credit union.

Ask around. If you have a job, ask other employees about a credit union that services those employed in the industry in which you work. Talk to your parents as well to see if they qualify to join local credit unions. You can also go to www.ncua.gov and www.creditunionsonline. com for information about credit unions in your area.

One large credit union is the USC Credit Union. All workers of the University of Southern California and all alumni of the school are eligible to join this credit union. Another large credit union is the North Jersey Federal Credit Union, which services employees in North Jersey who work in over 500 private and public institutions and corporations.

OPENING ACCOUNTS IN CREDIT UNIONS

To join a credit union, you must first be eligible and then you must own a share of the institution. When you deposit about $5 to $30 in a credit union account, you automatically own a share of the credit union.

For example, the USC Credit Union requires $10 to open a regular share savings account or $60 to open a regular share savings and checking account, but because there are fees associated with these small balances, most people would keep more cash in these accounts than the required minimums.

INSURANCE FOR CREDIT UNION ACCOUNTS

The National Credit Union Share Insurance Fund (NCUSIF) is the federal fund created by Congress in 1970 to insure members' deposits in credit unions up to the $100,000 federal limit. The NCUSIF is backed by the "full faith and credit" of the U.S. government just like FDIC insurance insures your deposits in banks. To make sure that your credit union is insured by NCUSIF, check www.ncua.gov.

7

Shopping for the Right Account

Now that we have described banks and credit unions and the basic products they offer, we will turn your attention to shopping for an account.

The *Truth in Savings Act*, a federal law, requires depository institutions like banks and credit unions to provide you with—or disclose to you—the important terms of their consumer deposit accounts. Institutions must tell you:

- The annual percentage yield and interest rate
- Cost information, such as fees that may be charged
- Information about other features such as any minimum balances required for earning interest or for avoiding fees

Institutions must give you, upon request, information about any account that institution offers. This will help you shop for the best accounts. You should get these disclosures before you actually open an account. In addition, the Truth in Savings Act generally requires that interest and fee information be provided on any statements that are sent to you about your account. If you have a rollover CD that is longer than one month, the law also requires that you get a renewal notice before the CD matures.

In the next section, we will discuss banks and credit unions with an online presence. Then we will give you a list of specific questions to ask any institution with which you are considering opening an account.

BANKS AND CREDIT UNIONS WITH AN ONLINE PRESENCE
Traditional Banks

Most major banks and credit unions have websites where you can get information about their services and fees. For example, Fleet Bank, Citibank, Chase Manhattan Bank, Bank of America, and Wells Fargo have had online banking for several years and are continually beefing up their web presence. Advantages of online banking include:

• *Convenience.* The ability to conduct transactions that you would ordinarily have to do in person at your bank (like moving money from one account to another), without leaving your home.

• *Online bill paying.* For most Teenvestors, online bill paying is probably not that important but just in case you need it, it's there for you.

Internet-Only Banks

Traditional banks with an Internet presence have been joined by Internet-only banks like EtradeBank and Netbank. Internet-only banks have emerged to offer consumers another outlet for saving or investing their money. Consider the following about Internet-only banks:

> **BOX 7.4**
> **A Handful of Major Traditional U.S. Banks**
>
> Citibank
> www.citibank.com
>
> Bank of America
> www.bankamerica.com
>
> Chase Manhattan Bank
> www.chase.com
>
> Wells Fargo
> www.wellsfargo.com
>
> Fleet Bank
> www.fleet.com

• *The benefit.* Internet-only banks often offer higher rates on bank products such as Certificates of Deposit and money market accounts. For example, at the time of this writing, EtradeBank was offering a five-year CD at an annual percentage rate of 4%, while Fleet and Bank of America (both traditional banks) were offering one for 3.24% and 3.10%, respectively.

• *The minor drawback.* The main drawback with Internet-only banks is that all interactions with the banks are done online since these banks don't have brick-and-mortar branches where customers can just drop by to bank or have their problems resolved.

> **BOX 7.5**
> **Young Americans Bank**
>
> The Young Americans Bank was founded in 1987 by Bill Daniels in Denver, Colorado. Its sole purpose is to provide affordable banking services to people less than 22 years old. The bank allows Teenvestors to open up savings accounts for as little as $10 and requires very low balances and fees for checking accounts and Certificates of Deposit compared to major banks. For more information, go to www.theyoungamericans.org.

In addition, all your deposits have to be mailed in to the bank. Finally, the online banks have been in existence for only two to six years as compared to traditional banks, some of which have been around for a century. However, in our view, the higher rates offered by these Internet only banks on their products make up for these minor inconveniences.

QUESTIONS AND CONSIDERATIONS WHEN OPENING AN ACCOUNT

Below is a list of questions that you will want to ask before opening an account:

- *The Interest Rate*

  - What is the annual percentage yield or interest rate?

  - Can the institution change the rate after you open the account?

  - Does the institution pay different levels of interest depending on the amount of your account balance?

- *Interest Compounding*

  - Does the bank pay simple or compounded interest on the account?

  - If the account pays compounded interest, how often is interest compounded? In other words, when does the insti-

46

BOX 7.7
How to Avoid Big Fees

Shop Around. Fees really do vary greatly from bank to bank. For example, at the time of this writing, the minimum balance required to be kept in regular savings accounts for Citibank and Chase in order to avoid fees (minimum balance requirements) were $500 and $400 respectively.

Use the Internet. Every major bank has a website where they post interest rates that they pay on their bank accounts, information on the minimum balance required in order to avoid fees, and other fees they charge you on accounts you establish with them.

Look for Special Fees. Look for special fee arrangements for very basic accounts. For example, some banks offer very basic accounts for beginning investors who don't conduct too many transactions a month.

Look for Low-Fee Custodial Accounts. Teenvestors should look for custodial accounts that offer low monthly fees or balances.

Use Your Parents' Bank. Banks in which your parents have their own accounts usually offer custodial accounts for Teenvestors for little or no fees and small minimum balances. For example, the Young Americans Bank specializes in accounts for Teenvestors and other young investors and savers. You can find out more about this bank by referring to Box 7.5 in this chapter. In addition, First Union, one of the top banks in the United States, has no monthly service charge on savings accounts for young people younger than 18 years old.

tution start paying interest on the interest you have already earned in the account?

- What is the minimum balance required before you begin earning interest?

• *Fees*

- Will you pay a flat monthly fee?

- Will you pay a fee if the balance in your account drops below a specified amount?

- Is there a charge for each deposit and withdrawal you make?

- If you can use ATMs to make deposits and withdrawals on your account, is there a charge for this service? Does it matter whether the transaction takes place at an ATM owned by the institution?

- Are fees reduced if you have other accounts at the institution?

Below is a list of specific questions that you will want to ask before opening a checking account:

• Will you be charged for each check you write? If so, how much?

• What is the charge for writing a check that bounces (a check returned for insufficient funds)? And what happens if you deposit a check written by another person, and it bounces? Are you charged a fee?

Below is a list of specific questions that you will want to ask before opening a CD:

• What is the term of the account? In other words, how long is it until the maturity date?

• Will the account roll over automatically? In other words, does the account renew if you do not withdraw your money at maturity (or during any grace period provided after maturity)? A *grace period* is the period after maturity when you can withdraw your money without penalty. If there is a grace period, how long is it?

• If you are allowed to withdraw your money before maturity, will the institution charge a penalty? If so, how much?

• Will the institution regularly send you the amount of interest you are earning on your account or regularly credit it to another account that you have with the institution (like a savings account)?

Below is a list of questions you will want to ask about other features:

• Does the institution have an online presence?

• Can you open accounts, pay bills, and do other transactions online?

• Does the institution allow parents of Teenvestors and other underage savers to open up custodial accounts with reduced fees?

• Does the institution limit the number or the dollar amount of withdrawals or deposits you make?

PART
3

Taking Stock

8

Look Before Diving into Stocks

A *stock* represents ownership in a company. Therefore, when you purchase stock, you become part owner of the company. The number of shares of a company's stock that you own generally indicates what portion of the company you own. For example, Walt Disney has sold 2,042,000,000 shares to the public. So if you owned ten shares of the company's stock, the percentage of the company you would own is .0000005% (10/2,042,000,000 = .0000005%). In general, companies sell stock to the public through a process called an *Initial Public Offering (IPO)* in order to get enough money to build their businesses.

Now, let's consider what a stock is not. When you purchase stock, you are investing in a company. This is very dif-

> **BOX 8.1**
> ### Number of Shares Issued by Select Companies*
>
> | | |
> |---|---|
> | General Electric | 10.0 Billion |
> | Microsoft | 5.3 Billion |
> | Wal-Mart | 4.4 Billion |
> | Ford | 1.8 Billion |
> | Ebay | 308.7 Million |
>
> *As of 1/6/03

BOX 8.2
Educational Websites* for Beginners

Teenvestor.com
www.teenvestor.com

SmartMoney
www.smartmoney.com

Teenanalyst.com
www.teenanalyst.com

Investorguide.com
www.investorguide.com

The Motley Fool
www.fool.com

The Vanguard Group
www.vanguard.com

Investopedia.com
www.investopedia.com

The Mutual Fund
Education Alliance
www.mfea.com

Morningstar
www.morningstar.com

NYSE
www.nyse.com

NASD
www.investor.nasd.com

About
stocks.about.com
mutualfunds.about.com

*For updates to this list, see www.teenvestor.com/top_websites.htm

---

ferent from when you purchase a corporate bond (see Chapter 3), in which you are lending money to a company. When you buy the stock of a company, there is no guarantee that you will get your money back or that your stock will go up in value. By contrast, when you purchase a corporate bond, you will be repaid unless the company goes bankrupt. Even if the company does go bankrupt, the company's lenders will get paid back first (with the proceeds of the sale of the company's assets) before the stockholders get a penny. Because those who own stock in a company take on more risk than those who lend money to the company, it's important that Teenvestors understand the basics of the stock market.

COMMON AND PREFERRED STOCK

There are two basic types of stocks:

• *Common stock*. Owning **common stock** entitles you to a share of a company's profit if the company decides to distribute those earnings by paying dividends. Common stockholders can also vote to determine a company's leadership and they can get a piece of the company's remaining value if it ever has to be sold due to bankruptcy.

• *Preferred stock*. **Preferred stock** generally pays a fixed rate of dividends. More important, the preferred stock dividends must be paid before common stockholders get their dividends. Because preferred stockholders get fixed dividends, they are not entitled to a larger share of the profits if the company does extremely well. On the other hand, they are taking on less risk because, if the company does poorly, they still get paid dividends before the common stockholders.

COMPANY SIZE

One of the ways investors classify companies is by size. The size of a company is important to investors because big companies are generally considered less risky (for example, safer) than tiny companies. This is because, as a rule of thumb, the value of the stock of a big company does not move up and down as quickly as the value of the stock of a small company. In addition, the profits of big companies generally don't grow or shrink as fast as the profits of small companies.

The size of a company is measured by its *market capitalization*, or

BOX 8.4
Advantages and Disadvantages of Common and Preferred Stock

	Advantages	Disadvantages
Common Stock	If the company makes money, the stockholders can benefit by receiving dividends if the company decides to distribute dividends.	If the company's profits go down, the stockholders may get no dividends at all and the value of their shares could go down.
Preferred Stock	Whether the company does well or not, the owner is entitled to dividends. Preferred stockholders also get paid before the common stockholders.	If the company's earnings go up, the owner gets only the promised dividends. Also, like common stockholders, if the company's profits go down, the value of their share of stock could also go down.

market cap, as it is commonly known. Market cap is the total market value of a company's outstanding stock and it can be calculated as follows:

BOX 8.5
Market Cap Categories*

Large-Cap
Over $10 billion in market cap

Mid-Cap
$2 to $10 billion in market cap

Small-Cap
$400 to $2 billion in market cap

Micro-Cap
Below $400 million in market cap

*These ranges are subjective and thus, depending upon who is the author, can vary. The values here represent the most common ranges for each category of market cap.

Price per Share
X
Number of Common
Shares Outstanding
=
Market Cap

Market caps are classified in four main categories: large-caps, mid-caps, small-caps, and micro-caps. We recommend that Teenvestors invest in large-cap and mid-cap stocks—at least for your first few stock purchases. For example, General Electric stock is considered a

BOX 8.6
Comparisons of Large-Cap and Small-Cap Companies

Market Cap	Is the stock price likely to increase or decrease suddenly?	Are the company profits likely to grow quickly?	Is it likely that the company will pay dividends?
Large-Cap	No	No	Yes
Small-Cap	Yes	Yes	No

large-cap stock. At the time of this writing, the market cap of General Electric was about $242 billion.

STOCK CATEGORIES

Besides large-cap, mid-cap, small-cap, and micro-cap stocks, investors classify companies by other categories that reflect their general nature. The more common classifications are briefly described below:

- *Blue-chip stocks* are high-quality stocks of large-cap companies that are considered financially sound and pay steady dividends. Since these stocks are considered safe, investors probably won't lose their money but, on the other hand, they won't make a killing in the market either. General Electric and IBM stocks are two examples of blue-chip stocks. An investment in blue-chip stocks should be the first stop for any beginning investor.

BOX 8.7
Five Typical Stock Categories

Blue-Chip
Growth
Income
Cyclical
Interest-Rate-Sensitive

- *Growth stocks* are stocks of relatively young companies with profits that grow quickly from year to year.

These stocks typically have higher earnings or revenue growth (15% or more) than blue-chip stocks but they are also riskier. Some growth stocks have little or no earnings but have a promising future as evidenced by growth in sales. An Internet-related stock such as Ebay is considered a growth stock—at least for now. Beginning investors generally like growth stocks, but we don't recommend them as your first investment.

• *Income stocks* are stocks of well-established companies that pay big dividends compared to the price that investors pay for the stocks. Investors in income stocks don't expect the value of their shares to go up very much but, on the other hand, these investors do expect to receive large steady dividends over a long period of time. Those who require a steady income, such as the retired, are likely to invest in income stocks. Institutions such as colleges also invest in these types of stocks because of their need for a safe and reliable source of income. Teenvestors don't typically invest in income stocks because these types of stocks generally don't increase very much in value over time compared to other stocks such as growth stocks or even blue-chip stocks. The stocks of utility companies are good examples of income stocks. See Box 8.8 for information on how investors measure dividends as compared to stock prices.

• *Cyclical stocks* are stocks of companies whose fortunes rise and fall with the health of the general economy. To some extent, all stocks are affected by the country's economic fluctuations, but stocks of some industries are more susceptible to the health of the economy than others. The value of these industries' stocks moves up and down with the economy more so than that of noncyclical companies because consumers often choose to delay buying expensive items like cars and houses until the economy improves. The chemical, steel, construction, automobile, real estate, and airline industries are examples of industries whose stocks are considered cyclical.

• *Interest-rate-sensitive stocks* are stocks that are affected by changes in interest rates. Companies in this category include banks and other financial institutions. In general, when interest rates are low (as is the case when the economy is in bad shape), banks typically don't make as much money as when interest rates are higher. A number of cyclical stocks are also interest-rate-sensitive stocks as the profitability of these companies is affected by interest rates.

INDUSTRY CATEGORY

Another way of classifying companies is by their *industry category*. An industry category is a way to group companies that have similar characteristics. In general, companies in the same industry prosper or decline together. For example, Ford and General Motors are in the automobile industry. As a general rule, if there is a decline in the price of Ford's stock, there will probably be a decline in the value of the stock price of General Motors.

One piece of advice that you will frequently get as a beginning investor is that you should diversify your portfolio. *Diversification* is the act of investing in several different industries or products so that a decline in the value of one investment does not affect the value of the other investments. In the stock market, diversification is achieved by investing in stocks of companies in different industries. For example, if your stock portfolio includes Ford, AOL-Time Warner, and Johnson & Johnson stocks (which are in the automobile, entertainment, and major drugs industries, respectively), a decline in the stock of one of the companies will not necessarily mean a decline in the stock of the other two because the other two companies sell completely different products and face different risks in the market.

A COMPANY'S OVERALL STRATEGY

Sometimes investors spend a lot of time digging for numbers that will give them an edge in deciding what stocks or investments to buy. Investment experts such as Warren Buffett and Peter Lynch believe that you should understand how a company makes its money before putting a penny into it. Can you explain what the company does? Have you seen or used the company's products? What sets the company apart from its competitors? Is the company clear about its strategic direction? Is the company dabbling in too many businesses? Is the company growing just by buying up other companies or is it truly gaining customers by offering good products or services? These are all questions that don't necessarily depend on any deep analysis to answer but are very important nonetheless.

Consider, for example, what Enron, Global Crossing, WorldCom, and Conseco have in common. For one thing, they have all filed for bankruptcy. For another thing, they have all grown quickly by acquiring other companies in the same industry. We believe that when companies go on acquisition binges, this can hide many financial problems that would otherwise be apparent. See Appendix I for more information on the Enron and WorldCom debacles.

THE STOCK MARKET INDEX

A *stock market index* tells you which direction the stock market is moving. Contrary to popular belief, you need not watch these indexes on a daily basis. Since we recommend making long-term investments, it stands to reason that the day-to-day movement of the market should not drive your investment strategy. We keep track of the following four indices:

- *The Teenvestor Index (published weekly—www.teenvestor.com)*
- *The Dow (published daily—www.djindexes.com)*

BOX 8.9
Select U.S. and International Stock Indices*
(Value as of 1/1/03 in Parentheses)

The Teenvestor Index (8,172.58)
www.teenvestor.com/indices.htm

The Dow (8,341.63)
www.djindexes.com

The S&P 500 (879.72)
www.spglobaldata.com

NASDAQ (1,335.51)
www.nasdaq.com

NASDAQ-100 (984.36)
www.nasdaq.com

The Russell 3000 (899.18)
www.russell.com

The Wilshire 5000 (8,343.19)
www.wilshire.com

TSX Composite Index (6,614.54)
Canada
www.tse.com

FTSE 100 (3,940.36)
United Kingdom
www.ftse.com

Hang Seng (9,321.29)
Hong Kong
www.hsi.com.hk

Nikkei 225 (8,578.95)
Japan
www.nni.nikkei.co.jp

DAX (2,892.63)
Germany
www.deutsche-boerse.com

*All are U.S. indices except where indicated.

- *The S&P 500 (published daily—www.spglobaldata.com)*
- *The NASDAQ (published daily—www.nasdaq.com)*

Long-term decline in the major indices is one of the things that tells you that the economy is not doing very well, as we explained in Chapter 3. Box 8.10 shows the historical rates of the the Dow, the S&P 500, the NASDAQ, and the Teenvestor Index from the end of 1989 to the end of 2002. Notice that the three major U.S. indices, namely the Dow, the S&P, and the NASDAQ, show consecutive losses from 2000 to 2002. Faced with these types of steady declines in marked indices, investors normally get more conservative in their investments. They typically move money from stocks to bonds or even to CDs and savings accounts. However, we feel that whether the economy is doing well or not, beginning investors

Historical Level of the Dow, the S&P 500, the NASDAQ, and the Teenvestor Index

(Figures Are for the Last Trading Day of Each Year)

	The Dow	% Change from Previous Year	S&P 500	% Change from Previous Year	NASDAQ	% Change from Previous Year	Teenvestor Index*	% Change from Previous Year
2002	8,341.6	−16.8%	879.8	−23.4%	1,335.5	−31.5%	8,172.6	−18.3%
2001	10,021.5	−7.1%	1,148.1	−13.0%	1,950.4	−21.1%	10,000.0	−
2000	10,786.9	−6.2%	1,320.3	−10.1%	2,470.5	−39.3%		
1999	11,497.1	25.2%	1,469.3	19.5%	4,069.3	85.6%		
1998	9,181.4	16.1%	1,229.2	26.7%	2,192.7	39.6%		
1997	7,908.4	22.6%	970.4	31.0%	1,570.4	21.6%		
1996	6,448.3	26.0%	740.7	20.3%	1,291.0	22.7%		
1995	5,117.1	33.5%	615.9	34.1%	1,052.1	39.9%		
1994	3,834.4	2.1%	459.3	−1.5%	752.0	−3.2%		
1993	3,754.1	13.7%	466.5	7.1%	776.8	14.7%		
1992	3,301.1	4.2%	435.7	4.5%	677.0	15.5%		
1991	3,168.8	20.3%	417.1	26.3%	586.3	56.8%		
1990	2,633.7	−4.3%	330.2	−6.6%	373.8	−17.8%		
1989	2,753.2	−	353.4		454.8	−		

*The Teenvestor Index was started in 2001; see www.teenvestor.com/indices.htm for updates to this table

should stay diversified and you should be invested in the strongest companies in the industry in which you are interested. We do not recommend moving in and out of specific investments depending on the economy because it is impossible to time the market. We have been around long enough to see the disasters that occurred with Internet and telecommunications companies to know that investment fads can get investors in trouble.

FINANCIAL MEASUREMENTS YOU SHOULD KNOW
Sales and Profit

Sales (also known as *revenue*) of a company represent how much money the company collects from its customers. *Profit* (also known as *earnings*) is how much a company keeps after subtracting expenses.

BOX 8.11
Description of Various U.S. Stock Indices

The Teenvestor Index. This is a weekly index established by a group of Teenvestors in 2002. It is made up of large companies that most Teenvestors recognize. See Box 8.12 for a list of the companies in our index. (See www.teenvestor.com/teenvestor_index.htm for more details on this index.)

The Dow Jones Industrial Average. Also known as the Dow, this is the most popular stock index. It is made up of 30 blue-chip stocks. Nearly all of the stocks are traded on the New York Stock Exchange, and you'd recognize most of the names in the index. See Box 8.12 for a list of the companies in the Dow. (See www.djindexes.com.)

The S&P 500. As the name suggests, this index is made up of 500 stocks. The stocks in this index are traded on the New York Stock Exchange (NYSE), the American Stock Exchange (AMEX), and the NASDAQ Exchange. Because the S&P 500 includes so many companies, some consider it a better gauge of how the market is doing than the Dow. (See www.spglobaldata.com.)

The NASDAQ Composite. The NASDAQ Composite Index is made up of the thousands of stocks traded on the NASDAQ Exchange. The NASDAQ Composite Index has traditionally reflected the movement of the value of small companies and of technology stocks. (See www.nasdaq.com.)

The NASDAQ 100. The NASDAQ 100 is made up of the top 100 nonfinancial companies in the NASDAQ stock market. It is different from the NASDAQ Composite Index, which is made up of nearly 5,000 companies. (See www.nasdaq.com.)

Russell 3000, Russell 2000, and Russell 1000. The Russell 3000 is an index made up of roughly 3,000 companies that collectively seeks to represent the whole U.S. stock market. The Russell 2000 Index is made up of the smallest 2,000 companies in the Russell 3000 Index. The Russell 1000 Index, on the other hand, is made up of the largest 1,000 companies in the Russell 3000 Index. (See www.russell.com.)

Wilshire 5000 Total Market. The Wilshire 5000 Total Market Index seeks to track the entire U.S. stock market. It actually contains more than 6,500 companies. (See www.wilshire.com.)

BOX 8.12
The Dow and the Teenvestor Index Components

Companies in the Dow	Companies in the Teenvestor Index
Alcoa	AOL-Time Warner, Inc.
American Express Co.	Boeing Co.
AT&T Corp.	Bristol-Myers Squibb Co.
Boeing Co.	Darden Restaurants
Caterpillar Inc.	Dell Computer Corp.
Citigroup Inc.	Ebay Inc.
Coca-Cola Co.	Exxon Mobil Corp.
Dupont Co.	Foot Locker, Inc.
Eastman Kodak Co.	Ford Motor Company
Exxon Mobil Corp.	Gap, Inc.
General Electric Co.	General Electric Co.
General Motors Corp.	Hershey Foods Corp.
Hewlett-Packard Co.	J.P. Morgan Chase & Co.
Home Depot	Kellogg Company
Honeywell Int'l Inc.	Kraft Foods, Inc.
Intel Corp.	McDonald's Corp.
IBM	McGraw-Hill Companies
International Paper Co.	Microsoft Corp.
J.P. Morgan Chase & Co.	Nokia Corporation
Johnson & Johnson	PepsiCo, Inc.
McDonald's Corp.	Procter & Gamble Co.
Merck & Co.	Prudential Financial, Inc.
Microsoft Corp.	Scholastic Corp.
Minnesota Mining &	Sears Roebuck and Co.
Manufacturing Co.	Sony Corporation
Philip Morris Cos.	Sprint PCS Group
Procter & Gamble Co.	Timberland Company
SBC Communications	Toys R US, Inc.
United Technologies Corp.	United Parcel Service
Walt Disney Company	Walt Disney Company
Wal-Mart Stores Inc.	

- *Formulas*: Money Collected from Customers = Sales
Sales–Expenses = Profit

- *Example 1*: If you had a business that you started for $500 and you sold $225 worth of items to customers, your sales would be the $225. However, your profit would not be $225 because you'd have to subtract what it cost you to make those sales to customers. If, for example, the items you sold to customers had cost you $125, your profit would have been $100.

- *Example 2*: The latest full-year sales at the time of this writing for General Electric were $126 billion and its profit was $14 billion.

Profit Margin

Profit Margin tells you how much a company made compared to how much it sold. In other words, a company's profit margin tells you what portion of the company's sales actually goes into its pockets. The higher the company's profit margin, the better.

- *Formula*: Profit ÷ Sales = Profit Margin

- *Example 1*: Using the previous example under "Sales and Profit," your profit in your business was $100 based on sales of $225. Your profit margin is calculated as follows:

$$\$100 \div \$225 = 44\%$$

- *Example 2*: The latest full-year profit margin at the time of this writing for General Electric was 11.2%.

Return on Equity

Return on equity (ROE) is just a fancy way to identify how much a company earns (also known as the company's *return*) compared to how much it invested to earn that money (also known as the company's *equity*).

- *Formula*: Profit ÷ Equity = ROE

- *Example 1*: If you had a business that you started for $500 (your equity) and you made $100 profit on that business every year, your return on equity would be $100 ÷ $500 or 20%. This means that you'd expect to make 20% of your initial investment in profit every year.

- *Example 2:* The latest full-year ROE at the time of this writing for General Electric was about 26%.

Earnings per Share

Earnings per share (EPS) indicates how much money the company earns for each share it has issued.

- *Formula*: Profit ÷ Number of Shares Outstanding = EPS

- *Example 1:* Suppose you start a business with a friend and you both share evenly in the profit of the company. This is the same as if your company issued two shares of stock—one to you and one to your friend. If you each invest $250 to start the company, each share is worth $250, making a total investment of $500. At the end of the year, if your company makes $100 profit, your partner will get $50 of the profit for his one share of stock and you'd get $50 of the profit for your share of stock. The earnings per share is then $50. In this example, profit is the $100 your company earns, and the number of common shares outstanding is equal to two— one share for you and another share for your partner (EPS = $100 ÷ 2 = $50).

- *Example 2:* The latest full-year EPS at the time of this writing for General Electric was about $1.40.

Price Earnings Ratio

Price earnings ratio (PE ratio) helps you assess how many years it will take to get back the investment you made in a company if the company's financial condition remains the same. It is viewed by some as an indication of how expensive a stock is to buy.

You will notice an inverse relationship between the EPS and PE ratios of a particular stock. When the EPS is small, the PE ratio is large because when calculating the PE ratio, the EPS goes in the denominator. Conversely, when the EPS is large, the PE ratio is small.

PE ratios are very high for new high-tech companies because many of them make very little money (if they make money at all). If a company makes no money at all, its PE ratio can't be calculated.

- *Formula*: Today's Price Per Share ÷ EPS = PE

- *Example 1*: In our description of EPS above, we assumed that you and your friend each invested $250 in your business. Remember, this is the same as buying a share of stock in a company for $250. We also assumed that you each made (or earned) $50 in profit for each share. To calculate your stock's PE ratio, you would take the $250 value of your share (price per share) and divide it by the $50 that you earned for each share of stock. The resulting PE ratio of five ($250 ÷ $50 = 5) means that it will take you five years to get back your initial investment of $250. This number is only meaningful if you use it for comparisons to the PE ratio of other companies in the same industry.

- *Example 2*: The latest average full-year PE ratio at the time of this writing for General Electric was about 29, and the average PE ratio of the companies in the S&P 500 is in the mid twenties.

Risk and Beta

Risk is a measure of how quickly the value of your investment can go up or down. As mentioned earlier, risk is higher for small-cap companies than for large-cap companies.

Beta measures how quickly a stock price moves up and down compared to the movement of a market index such as the S&P 500. In other words, beta tells you how much riskier your stock is compared to an investment in a hypothetical stock made up of all the components in the S&P 500. The higher the beta of a stock, the more risky the stock (as compared to the collective stocks in the S&P 500). In general, a beta of one is considered as safe as the total of all the companies in the market. Beta does not stay constant for a given stock over time. Box 8.15 gives a list of the betas of companies you may be familiar with.

• *Example 1*: If the value of the S&P 500 goes up by 10% from one day to the next, and your stock goes up by 10%, your stock is said to have a beta of one—the same beta of the market as represented by the S&P 500. This means that investing in your stock carries the same risk as investing, collectively, in the stocks in the S&P 500. If the value of the S&P 500 goes up by 10% from one day to the next, and your stock goes up by 20%, your stock is said to have a beta of two; it moves upward twice as much as the market as represented by the S&P 500. By the same token, it can also move down at the same pace, and this means that it carries a higher risk than that of the market.

• *Example 2*: The latest beta for General Electric at the time of this writing was 1.18. Therefore, you'd expect General Electric's stock to move up by 1.18% for each 1% increase in the S&P 500.

Investing in Stocks, Step by Step

STEP #1: FINDING A STOCK TO BUY

You have about 10,000 companies to choose from if you want to buy stocks. Researching each of these companies is an impossible task, so we have the following recommendations to get you started.

- *Begin with large-cap stocks.* All the stocks of companies in the list of the Dow Jones Industrial Average and most of the stocks in the Teenvestor Index (in Box 9.1 and Box 9.2, respectively) are large-cap stocks, which means they are stocks from some of the largest and most stable companies. In fact, at the time of this writing, the median market cap for companies in the Dow is about $51 billion—well above the $10 billion minimum level for large-cap stocks. You may also want to look at the large-cap stocks in the S&P 500 (www.spglobaldata.com).

BOX 9.1
The Companies in the Dow

Stock Name	Stock Symbol	Web Address
Alcoa	AA	www.alcoa.com
American Express Co.	AXP	www.americanexpress.com
AT&T Corp.	T	www.att.com
Boeing Co.	BA	www.boeing.com
Caterpillar Inc.	CAT	www.cat.com
Citigroup Inc.	C	www.citigroup.com
Coca-Cola Co.	KO	www.cocacola.com
Dupont Co.	DD	www.dupont.com
Eastman Kodak Co.	EK	www.kodak.com
Exxon Mobil Corp.	XOM	www.exxonmobil.com
General Electric Co.	GE	www.ge.com
General Motors Corp.	GM	www.gm.com
Hewlett-Packard Co.	HWP	www.hp.com
Home Depot	HD	www.homedepot.com
Honeywell Int'l Inc.	HON	www.honeywell.com
Intel Corp.	INTC	www.intc.com
IBM	IBM	www.ibm.com
International Paper Co.	IP	www.ipaper.com
J.P. Morgan Chase & Co.	JPM	www.chase.com
Johnson & Johnson	JNJ	www.jnj.com
McDonald's Corp.	MCD	www.mcdonalds.com
Merck & Co.	MRK	www.merck.com
Microsoft Corp.	MSFT	www.microsoft.com
Minnesota Mining & Manufacturing Co.	MMM	www.3m.com
Philip Morris Cos.	MO	www.philipmorris.com
Procter & Gamble Co.	PG	www.pg.com
SBC Communications	SBC	www.sbc.com
United Technologies Corp.	UTX	www.utc.com
Walt Disney Company	DIS	www.disney.com
Wal-Mart Stores Inc.	WMT	www.wal-mart.com

• *Consider stocks of companies in which you have a natural interest.* Look at large-cap stocks in industries you know something about or companies whose products you purchase frequently. Choose the companies that are leaders in that industry. A list of industry categories as determined by Multex Investor (www.

BOX 9.2
The Companies in the Teenvestor Index

Stock Name	Stock Symbol	Web Address
AOL-Time Warner, Inc.	AOL	www.aoltw.com
Boeing Co.	BA	www.boeing.com
Bristol-Myers Squibb Co.	BMY	www.squibb.com
Darden Restaurants	DRE	www.darden.com
Dell Computer Corp.	DELL	www.dell.com
Ebay Inc.	EBAY	www.ebay.com
Exxon Mobil Corp.	XOM	www.exxonmobil.com
Foot Locker, Inc.	Z	www.footlocker-inc.com
Ford Motor Company	F	www.ford.com
Gap, Inc.	GPS	www.gapinc.com
General Electric Co.	GE	www.ge.com
Hershey Foods Corp.	HSY	www.hersheys.com
J.P. Morgan Chase & Co.	JPM	www.chase.com
Kellogg Company	K	www.kelloggs.com
Kraft Foods, Inc.	KFT	www.kraft.com
McDonald's Corp.	MCD	www.mcdonalds.com
McGraw-Hill Companies	MHP	www.mcgraw-hill.com
Microsoft Corp	MSFT	www.microsoft.com
Nokia Corporation	NOK	www.nokia.com
PepsiCo, Inc.	PEP	www.pepsico.com
Procter & Gamble Co.	PG	www.pg.com
Prudential Financial, Inc.	PRU	www.prudential.com
Scholastic Corp.	SCHL	www.scholastic.com
Sears Roebuck and Co.	S	www.sears.com
Sony Corporation	SNE	www.sony.com
Sprint PCS Group	PCS	www.sprintpcs.com
Timberland Company	TBL	www.timberland.com
Toys R US, Inc.	TOY	www.toysrus.com
United Parcel Service	UPS	www.ups.com
Walt Disney Company	DIS	www.disney.com

multexinvestor.com) is shown in Box 9.3. While we happen to like the Multex Investor's list, there are many other stock categories established by other organizations such as Quicken and MSN Money Central that you can look at. To access the industry categories as determined by some of our favorite sites, go to www. teenvestor.com/industries.htm.

BOX 9.3
Industry Categories (by Multex Investor)

Advertising
Aerospace & Defense
Air Courier
Airline
Apparel/Accessories
Appliance & Tool
Audio & Video Equip.
Auto & Truck Manu-
facturers
Auto & Truck Parts
Beverages (Alcoholic)
Beverages (Non-Alc.)
Biotechnology &
Drugs
Broadcasting & Cable
Business Services
Casinos & Gaming
Chemical Manufact.
Chemicals—Plastics &
Rubber
Coal
Communications
Equipment
Communications Svc.
Computer Hardware
Computer Networks
Computer Peripherals
Computer Services
Computer Storage
Devices
Conglomerates
Constr. & Agric.
Machinery
Constr.—Supplies &
Fixtures
Construction—Raw
Materials
Construction Services
Consumer Financial
Services
Containers &
Packaging
Crops
Electric Utilities

Electronic Instr. &
Controls
Fabricated Plastic &
Rubber
Fish/Livestock
Food Processing
Footwear
Forestry & Wood
Products
Furniture & Fixtures
Gold & Silver
Health Care Facilities
Hotels & Motels
Insurance (Accident &
Health)
Insurance (Life)
Insurance (Miscella-
neous)
Insurance (Prop. &
Casualty)
Investment Services
Iron & Steel
Jewelry & Silverware
Major Drugs
Medical Equipment &
Supplies
Metal Mining
Misc. Capital Goods
Misc. Fabricated
Products
Misc. Financial Ser-
vices
Misc. Transportation
Mobile Homes & RVs
Money Center Banks
Motion Pictures
Natural Gas Utilities
Non-Metallic Mining
Office Equipment
Office Supplies
Oil & Gas—Integrated
Oil & Gas Operations
Oil Well Services &
Equipment

Paper & Paper
Products
Personal & House-
hold Prods.
Personal Services
Photography
Printing & Publishing
Printing Services
Railroads
Real Estate
Operations
Recreational Activities
Recreational Products
Regional Banks
Rental & Leasing
Restaurants
Retail (Apparel)
Retail (Catalog & Mail
Order)
Retail (Department &
Discount)
Retail (Drugs)
Retail (Grocery)
Retail (Home Improve-
ment)
Retail (Specialty)
Retail (Technology)
S&Ls/Savings Banks
Schools
Scientific & Technical
Instr.
Security Systems &
Services
Semiconductors
Software & Program-
ming
Textiles—Non-Apparel
Tires
Tobacco
Trucking
Waste Management
Services
Water Transportation
Water Utilities

• *Consider stocks in the industry in which your parents work or in which you work (if you have a job).* Your parents may be able to give you some insight as to the health of the companies in the industries in which they work. If you have a job, you may even learn about other companies in the same line of business. Keep in mind, however, that it is illegal to profit from *inside information*, information about a company that is not yet made available to the public. And don't, under any circumstances, invest all your money in one company's stock or in one industry, no matter how familiar you are with the company or industry.

• *Read current magazines and newspapers.* There are lots of publications that can help you come up with investment ideas. One of the most popular business publications is the *Wall Street Journal*, but there are other important business newspapers and magazines (see Box 9.4) that can help you gain some insight into the world of investing. We don't recommend that you rush out to buy stocks featured in these publications because we have found that, in general, by the time a big magazine or newspaper writes a glowing article about a company, that company's stock is overpriced. However, we do suggest that you read these publications to see the type of factors that the experts consider when recommending stocks. Once you understand what the experts look at, you can do your own research.

• *Check out online information.* The Internet is a great source of investment information. However, because of the sheer quantity of information, Teenvestors may find using it to do investment research a bit overwhelming. To help you get started, Box 9.5

> **BOX 9.4**
> **Publications for Researching Stocks**
>
> • *The Wall Street Journal*
> • *Investor's Business Daily*
> • *BusinessWeek*
> • *Business 2.0*
> • *Fortune*
> • *Forbes*
> • *Kiplinger's*
> • *Black Enterprise*
> • *Money*
> • *Better Investing*

BOX 9.5
Free Business News Websites*

CBS MarketWatch
www.cbsmarketwatch.com

CNBC
www.cnbc.com

CNN Money
money.cnn.com

The Street
www.thestreet.com

New York Times
www.nytimes.com

Bloomberg
www.bloomberg.com

Los Angeles Times
www.latimes.com

BusinessWeek Online
www.businessweek.com

Fortune
www.fortune.com

*For updates to site list, see www.teenvestor.com/top_websites.htm

shows a recommended list of websites with free registration that will help you sift through mountains of current business news.

Investing is not just about knowing what to do, but also about what pitfalls to avoid. We'll only touch upon a few in this section.

• *Avoid companies that gobble up lots of other companies.* You should avoid companies that have grown by buying a bunch of other companies. We've discovered that companies that grow in this way often have problems integrating the new companies into their own operations. And sometimes, buying these new companies has only served to hide some of the problems the acquiring company may have been having. See Box 9.6 for examples.

• *Avoid companies with too much debt.* Companies with lots of debt should also be avoided at all costs. How do you measure what's too much debt? If the debt is greater than the equity, stay away from the company unless the level of debt is typical of other companies in the same industry. You can find out all sorts of useful information about companies at the websites listed in Box 9.7.

• *Avoid Internet hype.* Internet chat group investment recommendations should be avoided at all costs, because you don't really know the motives of the individuals giving you investment advice.

BOX 9.6
Troubled Companies That Grew through Acquisitions

Enron	Filed for bankruptcy in 2002
WorldCom	Filed for bankruptcy in 2002
Global-Crossing	Filed for bankruptcy in 2002
Conseco	Filed for bankruptcy in 2002
Tyco	Questionable Bookkeeping Practices

Anyone with fingers to type can give their opinions about stocks, but be aware that sometimes the advice giver may actually benefit from promoting certain stocks—to your detriment. For a reminder of Internet scams by wayward Teenvestors, see Box 3.4 in Chapter 3.

STEP #2: GETTING BASIC INFORMATION

After deciding which company you may want to invest in, you should research some basic information:

- *Get the stock symbol.* With a stock symbol, you can get a quick summary of what a company does directly from financial websites. For example, the stock symbols of AT&T and General Electric are T and GE, respectively. For more information on stock symbols, go to our website, www.teenvestor.com/stock_symbols.htm.

- *Get a summary of what the company does.* Armed with a stock symbol, you can now get a basic summary about the company. Box 9.7 shows our list of the most important Internet sources of company information. Most of these websites have short summaries of the type of business in which each company is engaged. In addition, they can often tell you the main competitors of the

BOX 9.7
Websites for Researching Companies*

The SEC
www.sec.gov

Microsoft's Money Central
www.moneycentral.msn.com/investor

Multex Investor
www.multexinvestor.com

Hoover's
www.hoovers.com

Smart Money
www.smartmoney.com

Morningstar
www.morningstar.com

Netstockdirect
www.netstockdirect.com

Freeedgar
www.freeedgar.com

The Online Investor
www.theonlineinvestor.com

*For updates to site list, see
www.teenvestor.com/top_websites.htm

company you are researching. The website with the most comprehensive information is the Securities & Exchange Commission's website, www.sec.gov, but you may have a hard time wading through the documents filed by the companies that give detailed accounting of their businesses. As a start, go to the other sites first for basic company information. For more information on how to get the information you need from these websites, go to www.teenvestor.com/research.htm.

• *Go to the company's website.* By now, all large companies have their own websites. Boxes 9.1 and 9.2, presented earlier, show a list of the Dow and the Teenvestor Index components and their websites. You can usually get a lot of information about what these companies do from their websites. In addition, you can get copies of their annual reports from their sites (usually in PDF format so you'll need a free copy of Acrobat Reader installed on your computer). We find that it isn't always easy to locate the annual reports on corporate websites. Look for the sections in the company's websites typically labeled "Investor Relations," "Investors," "About Us," or "Investors." If all else fails, use the search feature on the companies' websites to look for "annual reports."

- *Request a hard copy of the company's annual report.* Call the investor relations department of the company that interests you. You can get the appropriate phone numbers from the company's website.

STEP #3: DOING YOUR RESEARCH

More thorough research may be required for companies that are smaller and not so well known. At the very least, you should get the key data you need for your evaluation from websites listed in Box 9.7. For further details on how to obtain this data, go to www.teenvestor.com/research.htm. Key financial data you should consider when researching a stock are:

- *Sales and profit.* Find out how sales and profit have been growing or changing over the past five years. Ideally, you want to see an average growth in sales of 10% or more for large-cap companies and 15% or more for mid- to small-cap companies. The same goes for growth in profit or earnings. Keep in mind, however, that during difficult economic times (as the country experienced after the September 11, 2001, attacks on the World Trade Center and the Pentagon), few companies can meet the lofty goals we just described regarding growth of sales and profit. For this reason, it is better to compare the performance of the company relative to other companies in the same industry.

- *Profit margin (profit/sales).* Trends in profit margin can tell you whether a company is getting stronger or dete-

> **BOX 9.8**
> **The Data You Need to Do More In-Depth Research***
>
> - Sales and Profit
> - Profit Margin
> - Return on Equity (ROE)
> - Earnings per Share (EPS)
> - Price Earnings Ratio
> - Beta
>
> *To find out how to get this data on any stock, go to www.teenvestor.com/research.htm

riorating. Look for a profit margin that has continued to grow steadily.

• *Return on equity (profit/equity).* You want a trend that shows that the company's return on equity (ROE) is getting bigger or at least is not shrinking. Comparing the company's ROE to those of its competitors may be helpful.

• *Earnings per share (profit/shares outstanding).* This can tell you whether the company is making more money each year for the common shareholders.

• *Price earnings ratio (stock price/earnings per share).* The price earnings ratio gives you an indication of how expensive a stock is relative to how much it earns. There are those who believe that a company's PE ratio may fluctuate but that it reverts back to a constant level. The average PE ratio for the companies in the S&P 500 is in the mid twenties. Relatively young technology companies generally have stocks with high PE ratios because they have very low earnings. For this reason, PE ratios for these types of companies are not meaningful. If the PE ratio has increased dramatically over, say, a three-year period, this may be an indication that the stock is too expensive. Once again, a comparison of the PE ratio of stocks in the same industry may give you some insight into the company you are evaluating.

• *Beta.* Beta is an indication of the riskiness of a stock. As a beginning investor, we suggest that you invest in companies whose betas are 1.5 or less.

• *Stock price.* It makes sense to look at how the stock prices have changed over the past one, two, three, and five years. Fortunately, you can get a graph of any company's stock price from free websites listed in Box 9.9. Our favorite stock charting site is www.bigcharts.com. If you see any unusual dips in a stock's price, you should find out whether that company in particular is having problems or whether the whole industry (or the entire stock market) is in bad shape at the time.

So far, we have focused on just looking at the financial trends in a single company you have chosen to evaluate. But to make your analysis complete, you should compare the financial data in one company to the financial data of one or two of its competitors.

STEP #4: SET UP A DUMMY PORTFOLIO

Setting up a dummy portfolio is one way you can overcome the fear of taking that first step in investing. A *dummy portfolio* is a group of stocks you pretend to buy. No money actually changes hands, but you get a chance to practice picking stocks and following their progress. There are lots of websites that allow you to set up dummy portfolios so you can try your hand at investing. Portfolios set up on these websites get recalculated every day to tell you exactly how much you have made or lost on your investments. We list a few websites where you can set up your own pretend portfolio in Box 9.10. For nearly all these sites, you have to register (for free) in order to use their portfolio services.

> **BOX 9.10**
> **Websites for Setting Up Dummy Portfolios***
>
> Quicken
> www.quicken.com
>
> Yahoo!Finance
> finance.yahoo.com
>
> Wall Street City
> www.wallstreetcity.com
>
> ClearStation
> www.clearstation.com
>
> Microsoft's Money Central
> www.moneycentral.msn.com
>
> Lycos
> finance.lycos.com
>
> SmartMoney
> www.smartmoney.com
>
> *For more information, see
> www.teenvestor.com/dummy_portfolio.htm

STEP #5: FINDING AN ONLINE BROKER

Most stock purchases are handled through a *broker*, a professional who handles your stock purchases and sales for a fee. These fees can vary widely. Most Teenvestors can't afford to go to full-service brokers to buy or sell stock, but online brokers are usually a cheap alternative. Here are some things you should know about the more inexpensive online brokers you are likely to find:

• There are two types of online brokers: basic and speciality. Basic online brokers are the most affordable online brokers that we can find. You should look into the services of the brokers in Box 9.11. They generally offer low-cost basic trading services, low minimum balance requirements, and low inactivity fees. For example, Firstrade and Trading Direct charge $6.95 and $9.95 respectively for buying and selling shares and they have no minimum balance requirements although they charge an inactivity fee if they determine that you are not an active trader. Please bear in mind that online brokers change their commission, fee, and balance requirement schedules all the time so you have to go to their websites for up-to-date information. You can also go to our website, www.teenvestor.com/top_websites.htm for an updated list of recommended brokers. Box 9.12 is a comparison of fees charged by the basic online brokers.

Sharebuilder, BUYandHOLD, and Folifn are specialty online

BOX 9.12
Details on Basic Affordable Online Brokers

	Minimum Balance to Open Account	Basic Market Order Trading Cost	Inactivity Fee per Year/ Account Maintenance Fee per Year*
Firstrade	None	$6.95	$35
Trading Direct	None	$9.95	$50
Scottrade	$500	$7.00	None
Mydiscountbroker.com	$1,000	$12.00	$60
Brokerage America	$1,000	$5.00	None
TD Waterhouse	$1,000	$14.95	$80
Etrade	$1,000	$14.99	$100
Ameritrade	$2,000	$10.99	$60

*Inactivity fee is charged if you don't trade a certain number of times during a given period. Account maintenance fee is charged if your account is below a certain balance. See www.teenvestor.com/brokers.htm for updates.

brokers that charge as little as $4 per trade. For the low fees, these companies generally purchase shares for you twice a day as opposed to purchasing shares for you as soon as you put in your order. This is just fine for Teenvestors since you should only buy stocks that don't fluctuate too much. These brokers also allow you to buy fractions of a share. Box 9.13 gives more details of the features of these specialty brokers.

• Teenvestors should know the difference between a *market order* and a *limit order*. If you want the broker to buy a stock for you at whatever price at which that stock is being sold, this is called a market order. On the other hand, if you tell the broker that you don't want to pay more than a certain amount for a stock, this is called a limit order. Limit orders cost more than market orders. You would request limit orders for stocks that move up and down quickly (that is, stocks with a high beta).

Find out what your broker charges for each type of order. The difference between market and limit orders can be as much as $5 for some online brokers. As a beginning investor, you should buy

---

BOX 9.13
Details on Specialty Online Brokers
(In Order of Preference as Determined by Teenvestor.com)

All specialty brokers listed below allow you to invest in fractions of a share. In addition, they all generally buy shares for you twice a day, not as soon as you put in your order. Besides that, each one has a different price structure.

Sharebuilder

Sharebuilder allows you to buy stocks for a $4 commission per transaction but charges $15.95 in commission to sell your shares. If you want to choose the subscription option of $12 per month, you can buy all the shares you want. You will still have to pay $15.95 to sell, however. Sharebuilder has no investment minimums and no inactivity fees. (See www.sharebuilder.com for more information.)

FolioFn

FolioFn also allows you to buy stocks for a $4 commission per transaction but charges $14.95 in commission to sell shares. If you subscribe for $14.95 per month, you can make up to 500 free trades, both buying and selling. The most attractive feature of FolioFn is that you can actually create your own basket of stocks, much like mutual funds, through their Folio Investing platform. FolioFn has no investment minimums and no inactivity fees. (See www.foliofn.com for more information.)

BUYandHOLD

BUYandHOLD has a subscription plan only. You can pay $6.99 per month, which allows you to make two buy or two sale transactions. Alternatively, if you pay per month, you can buy or sell as many shares as you want each month. BUYandHOLD has no investment minimums and no inactivity fees. (See www.buyandhold.com for more information.)

---

stocks that are stable (for example, low beta stocks) at least for your first few transactions. In this way, you can put in market orders without the fear of the stock price increasing on you by the time your online broker processes your transaction.

• *There may be extra charges for services*. Online brokers often disclose all their charges on their websites. However, we've found that you often have to look hard to find these fees. Some charges you should look for are charges for being inactive (for example, not being an active trader), falling below a minimum balance, having a statement mailed to you, speaking to a live person, mailing your stock certificates, and listing the stock in your name instead of in the "street name" (as we will discuss further in the next chapter).

STEP #6: OPENING A BROKERAGE ACCOUNT

For most online brokers, you have the option of applying online for a brokerage account or printing out an application and mailing it in with a check to establish your account. To open an account, here are a few things you need to know:

- *Account types*. There are several varieties of accounts you can open with an online broker. The most common accounts are:

  - *An individual account*. This is an account established by a person who is not a minor.

  - *A joint account*. This is an account established by two individuals, normally a husband and wife, but it can be opened by any two people who are not minors.

  - *A custodial account*. This is an account typically opened for a minor by an adult who is serving as the custodian for the account. The actual owner of the account is the minor but he can't take control of the account until he is no longer a minor (for example, until he is at least 18 years old in most states). Parents typically open this type of account for their children.

  - *A retirement account (such as an IRA)*. This is an account established for retirement purposes in order to take advantage of tax breaks offered by the government. We will discuss retirement accounts and IRAs in a later chapter.

  - *An education savings account*. This is an education savings account, properly known as the Coverdell Educational Savings Account, with tax benefits.

• *Information you may be asked to give.* Here are some of the pieces of information you may be asked to put on a brokerage account application:

▪ **Your bank account information.** This is necessary, especially if you want to transfer money from your bank account to a brokerage account and vice versa. Bank account information may include your bank's routing number, which are the series of numbers on the bottom of your personal checks.

▪ **Your Social Security number.** Of course, you will also need your Social Security number. If your parents are opening a custodial account for you, you will also need to have your own Social Security number.

STEP #7: GET ON A STEADY BUYING PROGRAM

No one can predict how stock prices will move. This fact will never, ever change despite how many people think they are investing geniuses. Does this mean that you don't do any research on the stock you want to buy? Of course not! You always have to look at how much money a company has made in the past, how much it is likely to make in the future, and how much in demand its product may be in the future. However, in the short term, you can't tell when a stock will dip in price or increase in price. For this reason, most experts recommend that you give up the idea of guessing the direction of the price of any stock. If you start investing by buying large, reliable companies (such as the ones on the Dow), you can probably assume that most of them will be decent investments over the long haul. They won't make you rich overnight, but they are good ways to get started as an investor. The experts recommend that when you find strong companies you want to own over a long period of time, you use a technique called ***dollar cost averaging***.

The idea behind dollar cost averaging is that you should invest the same dollar amount in a stock each period no matter how the stock price changes, as long as you still have confidence in the strength of the company. For example, if you have $100 to invest in a stock each month, you buy as many shares of one stock as you can with that money. If the stock price was $20 in one month, you'd purchase five shares ($100/$20 = 5). If the stock price was $25 on another month, you'd buy four shares ($100/$25 = 4). If you purchase stocks like this over a long period of time, you are likely to get a favorable average stock price if the long-term prospect of the company is good. Online brokers like Shapebuilder and Buy And Hold have programs in which you can invest the same dollar amount in specific stocks each month. (See www.teenvestor.com/dca.htm for more information.)

STEP #8: KEEP ALL YOUR RECORDS

To save yourself the headache of dealing with the IRS on your taxes, we recommend that you follow the following good record-keeping procedures:

- *Save all your orders*. Keep good records of what you buy from your broker each time you make a purchase, including how much you paid in commissions.

- *Save your confirmations*. Every time you buy from your broker online, you will get a confirmation. Keep this confirmation as well. Don't throw *anything* out when it comes to your dealings with the stock market. This will save you a lot of hassles at tax time.

- *Ask for a statement*. Chances are that you will receive a statement of all your transactions when you make them. If possible, try to get a year-end statement that shows all your transactions during the year. It may cost you extra with deep-discount brokers, but it is worth it.

Buying Stock Directly at the Source

The ability to purchase stock directly from companies without a broker is one of the most useful investment tools for Teenvestors. Purchasing stocks directly can be an effective way of building your stock portfolio over a long period of time—especially if you have little cash at your disposal. There are two types of direct investment plans: direct stock plans (DSPs) and dividend reinvestment plans (DRIPs).

Teenvestors generally know very little (if anything at all) about direct investment plans. Since these plans allow investors to purchase stocks directly from companies, it's not to the advantage of brokers to encourage investors to invest in them on their own. To bring you up to speed on these products, this chapter covers concepts, benefits, and disadvantages of investing in DSPs and DRIPs.

> **BOX 10.1**
> **Why Buy Stocks without a Broker?**
>
> - You won't have to pay as much in fees.
> - You can buy fractions of a share.
> - You can automatically reinvest your dividends.

89

WHY COMPANIES SELL STOCKS DIRECTLY TO YOU

Thousands of companies have found ways to allow investors an opportunity to purchase shares directly. They like direct investment plans for several reasons:

- *They build customer loyalty.* Selling stock directly to the public is one way companies can extend the reach of their businesses since shareholders make loyal customers.

- *They encourage long-term investing.* Investors in DSPs and DRIPs are typically small investors. Small investors are generally long-term investors who are unlikely to sell their stocks when the market dips a bit.

- *They provide a cheaper source of financing.* Companies that offer direct investing plans find it cheaper to raise money directly from investors without having to go through the legal expense of doing a formal stock offering to the public (for example, without having to do an Initial Public Offering).

THE DIFFERENCE BETWEEN DSPS AND DRIPS

Companies sometimes call their direct investment plans by different names. No matter what they call them, it's important that you understand the distinction between the two different types of direct investment plans. Below are the specific descriptions of what constitutes a DSP and a DRIP.

- *DSPs.* Companies that allow you to buy *your first share and all other shares* from them directly are said to have **direct purchase plans DSPs.** These types of plans are sometimes called **no-load stock** or **no-load share plans.** To avoid confusion with the various names given to these plans, just remember that when we discuss

DSPs, we are referring to plans that allow you to buy your first share (and all other shares) from the company directly.

• *DRIPs.* Dividend reinvestment plans (*DRIPs*) are very similar to DSPs except that DRIPs can only be purchased when *you already own at least one registered share of the company.* What this means is that you can only participate in a company's DRIP if you are a *shareholder of record.* Being a shareholder of record means that the company whose stock you have purchased has your name in its records as an owner of the stock (see Box 10.3). By contrast, to participate in a DSP, you don't have to be a shareholder of record because, as we noted earlier, you can buy your first share directly from the company.

There are only about 300 companies that offer DSPs, including large organizations such as IBM, General Electric, McDonald's, Exxon, Procter & Gamble, Sears, Wal-Mart, J.C. Penney, and many others. Many more companies—more than 1,100—however, offer DRIPs. Some companies—such as McDonald's and Exxon Mobil—offer both DSPs and DRIPs.

ADVANTAGES AND DISADVANTAGES OF DSPS AND DRIPS

DSPs and DRIPs are great for small investors for the following reasons:

• *Teenvestors can afford it.* DSPs and DRIPs allow Teenvestors to get into the stock market cheaply. Many companies with DSPs and

BOX 10.3
Becoming a Shareholder of Record

Becoming a **shareholder of record** is something you will have to do in order to be able to buy stock directly from companies. Normally, when you buy shares through a full-service broker such as Merrill Lynch or through an online broker such as Etrade, the shares you buy are registered in the broker's name, or *street name* as it is called. So, for example, if you buy a share of General Motors (GM) through Etrade, the broker will register the purchase in Etrade's name (the street name). GM will not know that you actually own the stock because as the stock is not registered in your name, you are not a shareholder of record. All GM knows is that Etrade has bought shares on someone's behalf. As a practical matter, it is only important whether your shares are registered in your name or in the street name if you want to participate in a DRIP because you must be the owner of record of at least one share of stock in order to participate in the company's DRIP program. If you don't care about buying shares through DRIPs, you would not need to make sure that you are the shareholder of record.

Let's assume for now that you have already bought a share of GM from an online broker and your share was registered in the street name. In order to participate in DRIPs, you'd have to transfer the registration to your name (thereby becoming the shareholder of record) and have your broker send your stock certificate to you. The certificate is the ultimate proof that you own stock in GM and it is also what gets your name on GM's list of who owns its stock.

Unfortunately, when a broker transfers stock in your name and issues you a stock certificate, they usually charge you from $15 to $25—but some charge as much as $75. However, this may be a small price to pay to begin participating in DRIPs because, once you are a registered owner of a share of a participating company's stock, you can invest in the stock periodically when you feel like it and at very little cost.

BOX 10.4
Summary of Advantages and Disadvantages of Stock Purchase Plans

Advantages:
- They are affordable.
- The fees are low.
- Dividend reinvestment is allowed.

Disadvantages:
- They require good record keeping.
- The exact timing of share purchases and selling is controlled by the company, not you.
- The minimum required investment is high in some cases—McDonald's requires $500 minimum first purchase.

DRIPs allow you to make additional share purchases (full or fractional shares) with as little as $10 once you join their plans. After opening the account, you can invest as little or as much as you want. In fact, you can buy fractions of a share of stock if you don't have enough money to buy a full share (after you have met the company's initial purchase requirement).

For example, imagine that one share of Incredible Productions goes for $500 and that you are an investor with only $50 to invest. You don't own any shares of this company but you would really like to start investing in it. If you already have the good fortune to own a share of Incredible Productions and assuming that the company offers DRIPs or DSPs to investors, you could purchase a fraction of one share representing a one-tenth ($50 ÷ $500 = 1/10th) ownership interest of one share.

• *Fees are low.* Compared to the typical broker, the fees for investing in DSPs and DRIPs are very low. There is usually a one-time initial set-up fee of $5 to $15 for an account. Some of these plans charge as little as 3 to 15 cents in fees for each purchase of stock, while others charge $2 and up.

• *The plans allow dividend reinvestments.* Stocks pay dividends every three months. Instead of pocketing that money, you can have the plan reinvest it in the company's stock. If you know anything about the power of compounding (as described in Chapter 2), you know that reinvested money can earn you higher returns on a compounded basis.

DSPs and DRIPs also have their disadvantages:

• *Record keeping.* You have to keep good records of any purchases you make through these plans because the dividends are considered taxable income even if you reinvest them. In addition, when you sell your shares, you need records showing how much you paid for your shares so you can calculate how much money you made (called *capital gains*) for tax purposes. It's likely that if you are a Teenvestor under 14 years old, you will probably owe no taxes whereas, if you are over 14 years of age, you may have to pay taxes on dividends and on profits when you sell your shares.

• *You don't control timing of share purchases and sales.* You can only buy or sell shares for your DSPs and DRIPs on specific dates that are determined by the companies offering these plans. For example, some companies may only buy or sell stocks for you once a week, while others may buy or sell stocks for you once a month or even once every three months. This means that if stock prices are moving around a lot, you can never tell the price at which you will end up buying or selling the stock. This shouldn't really be a big problem for most Teenvestors if you are investing, as we recommend, in big, stable, large-cap companies whose stock prices don't fluctuate that much.

BOX 10.5
GE's Stock Purchase Plan (A DSP and DRIP Plan)

Since a real example is always better than talking in hypothetical terms, we'll use the General Electric plan (the GE Stock Direct Plan) to show you the various features of the direct investment plan. By using GE as an example, we are not necessarily recommending the company's stock. You should decide which stock to buy based on your analysis of the fundamentals. Keep in mind, also, that each direct investment plan has its own special requirements, so you will want to get copies of the plan documents and read them carefully. They are easy to read and understand.

GE's plan offers both a DSP and DRIP. You can buy your first share from the company when you enroll or you can enroll if you already own a share in your name.

Minimum Initial Investment

The minimum investment depends on whether you already own GE stock in your own name (as opposed to the street name) or not. If you own stock registered in your own name, you can participate in GE Stock Direct without being required to make a minimum investment or incurring any fees. If you don't already own a share of GE stock, you need $250 plus a registration fee of $7.50 in order to participate in the plan.

Dividend Reinvestment

The GE Stock Direct Plan allows you, at no extra cost, to reinvest your dividends in GE stock if you choose to do so.

Optional Cash Investments

As long as you have established an account with GE Stock Direct, you can invest any amount from $10 to $10,000 each week. Since GE stock sells for considerably more than $10, a $10 investment will get you a fraction of a share. You will be charged a small fee ($1–$3) for each additional investment that you make.

Selling Shares

You can sell shares in your GE account for a transaction fee of $10 plus 15 cents for each share you sell. The fees will be deducted automatically from the money you get for the sale.

(continued)

Gifts

If you are enrolled in GE Stock Direct, you can give GE stock as a gift but you must first open an account for the recipient of the stock gift. In order to open up an account, you can transfer your own shares to the new account or you can transfer cash to the account.

• *In some cases, the minimum investment amount can be high.* Even though there are some companies that require small initial investments of only $100, many companies require much higher initial investments. For example, McDonald's has an initial investment minimum of $500. You should expect an average required minimum investment of about $300, however.

• *Becoming a shareholder of record can be expensive.* Becoming a shareholder of record can be expensive depending on which broker you use to make your initial purchase of stock. One discount online broker we know charges $75 to transfer stock from the street name to a person's name. The typical charge, however, is between $15 and $25, but you have to shop around for the best record transfer rates.

Direct Investment Plans, Step by Step

STEP #1: FINDING COMPANIES WITH DIRECT INVESTMENT PLANS

• *Look for large-cap companies with direct investment plans.* To find DRIPs and DSPs, you should first look at large-cap stocks. You may recall that the median market cap of the companies in the Dow is currently about $51 billion so you may want to start with the Dow. Box 11.1 shows which companies in the Dow have direct investment plans and the phone numbers to call for more information. Appendix II gives more details about the direct investment plans of the companies in the Dow. Note that all the companies in the Dow have a direct investment program except for Citigroup, Hewlett-Packard, and Microsoft. There are more than 1,400 companies with direct investment plans, so your search for suitable companies should not end with the Dow. You may also want to

BOX 11.1

The Direct Investment Contact Information for the Dow Companies

Stock Name (Symbol)	Web Address	Phone Number for Plan Materials
Alcoa (AA)	www.alcoa.com	800-317-4445
American Express Co. (AXP)	www.americanexpress.com	800-842-7629
AT&T Corp. (T)	www.att.com	800-348-8288
Boeing Co. (BA)	www.boeing.com	888-777-0923
Caterpillar Inc. (CAT)	www.cat.com	800-446-2617
Citigroup Inc. (C)	www.citigroup.com	No Plan
Coca-Cola Co. (KO)	www.cocacola.com	888-265-3747
Dupont Co. (DD)	www.dupont.com	888-983-8766
Eastman Kodak Co. (EK)	www.kodak.com	800-253-6057
Exxon Mobil Corp. (XOM)	www.exxonmobil.com	800-252-1800
General Electric Co. (GE)	www.ge.com	800-786-2543
General Motors Corp. (GM)	www.gm.com	800-331-9922
Hewlett-Packard Co. (HWP)	www.hp.com	No Plan
Home Depot (HD)	www.homedepot.com	877-HD-SHARE
Honeywell International Inc. (HON)	www.honeywell.com	800-647-7147
Intel Corp. (INTC)	www.intc.com	800-298-0146
IBM (IBM)	www.ibm.com	888-426-6700
International Paper Co. (IP)	www.ipaper.com	800-678-8715
J.P. Morgan Chase & Co. (JPM)	www.chase.com	800-758-4651
Johnson & Johnson (JNJ)	www.jnj.com	800-328-9033
McDonald's Corp. (MCD)	www.mcdonalds.com	800-621-7825
Merck & Co. (MRK)	www.merck.com	800-831-8248
Microsoft Corp. (MSFT)	www.microsoft.com	No Plan
Minnesota Mining & Manufacturing Co. (3M)	www.3m.com	800-401-1952
Philip Morris Cos. (MO)	www.philipmorris.com	800-442-0077
Procter & Gamble Co. (PG)	www.pg.com	800-764-7483
SBC Communications (SBC)	www.sbc.com	800-351-7221
United Technologies Corp. (UTX)	www.utc.com	800-519-3111
Walt Disney Co. (DIS)	www.disney.com	818-553-7200
Wal-Mart Stores Inc. (WMT)	www.wal-mart.com	800-438-6278

look into the companies in the Teenvestor Index (www.teenvestor. com) or the S&P 500 (www.spglobaldata.com).

- *Use helpful websites.* Box 11.2 lists websites that will help you find companies that offer DRIPs and DSPs. These websites can also tell you about investment minimums and give you other useful information about direct investment plans. In addition, some of them have information for the following categories of companies with direct investment plans:

- Companies in the Dow

- Companies in the Fortune 500 list

- Companies in the Forbes 500 list

- Companies in the S&P 500

DripAdvisor (shown in Box 11.2) gives you an alphabetical listing of direct investment plans and allows you to sort by the number of shares to qualify, minimum investment balances, and other criteria. We strongly recommend that you start investing in direct investment plans by getting into plans that don't require that you already own a share. Equiserve and Mellon Investor Services provide services to companies with direct investment plans so you can get information on many of these plans through their websites.

> **BOX 11.2**
> **Websites for Companies that Offer DRIPs and DSPs***
>
> Netstockdirect
> www.netstockdirect.com
>
> DirectInvesting.com
> www.directinvesting.com
>
> Drip Advisor
> www.dripadvisor.com
>
> Equiserve
> www.equiserve.com
>
> Mellon Investor Services
> www.melloninvestor.com
>
> *For updates on new sites, see
> www.teenvestor.com/drips.htm

- *Check the company website.* If you have any companies in mind, you can always check their website to see if they offer a direct investment plan. Look for sections on the sites that refer to "investors," "investor relations," or "shareholder services." If all else fails, do a search on the website to look for references to "dividend reinvestment plan" or "dividend investment plan."

STEP #2: RESEARCH YOUR COMPANY

Follow the same guidelines we discussed in Chapter 9 on how to identify good investment prospects. At the very least, call the company to get a copy of their annual report. In addition, you can get information about the company from the SEC website, www.sec.gov, if you know its stock symbol. The websites in Box 9.7 also give you links to company summaries and stock-price charts.

The websites in Box 11.2 will help you get detailed information about specific direct investment plans. For some companies that offer direct investment plans, you can even order the plan materials online at no charge. At the very least, you will be able to contact the companies through the phone numbers provided by these websites.

STEP #3: BECOME AN OWNER OF RECORD IF NECESSARY

If the direct investment plan you are interested in is of the DSP variety that allows you to buy your first share of stock from the company, you can move on to Step #4. If, however, you need to be the owner of record (in other words, you need a stock certificate to be issued in your name) before you can make a purchase, then you will probably have to buy a share of the company's stock through a discount online broker or through companies (see Box 11.3) that specialize in helping people interested in direct investment plans buy one share (or just a few shares). MoneyPaper's Temper Enrollment Service and the NAIC's Own a Share of America Program will purchase a share (or a few

BOX 11.3
Services that Can Help You Buy a Few Shares Registered in Your Name

Money Paper's Temper Enrollment Service
800-295-2550
www.moneypaper.com

NAIC's Own a Share of America Program
www.better-investing.org

First Share
www.firstshare.com

shares) and register it in your name for a fee. Another company, First-Share, is a member organization that depends on members to provide each other with shares for the purpose of participating in direct investment plans. We recommend that you only use these share-buying services if you find that online brokers charge too much for share transfers.

Remember that after you buy a share through a broker, the stock is not in your name—it is in the street name or the name of the broker. To participate in some direct investment plans, you must then have the broker transfer the stock certificate to your name and have it mailed to you.

You can also get stock as a gift from a plan participant. Many direct investment plans make it easy for a participant to transfers shares to someone else as a gift. If you know someone in a direct investment plan, ask him or her to contact the plan administrator for the transfer forms. Once you are registered as the owner of the gift stocks, you can buy more shares in the plan. If you have parents or relatives who work with full-service brokers, they may be able to get their brokers to transfer a few of their shares to your name.

STEP #4: ORDERING THE APPLICATION

For the direct investment plans that don't have online applications, you can order an application by calling the *plan administrator*. The plan administrator is usually another organization that the company offering the plan hires to take care of the paperwork associated with opening up accounts. The plan administrator for General Electric, for example, is Bank of New York. Through the websites in Box 11.2, you can order applications for many direct investment plans. The phone numbers listed in Box 11.1 are for the Dow companies' plans administrators.

STEP #5: FILLING OUT THE APPLICATION

All direct investment plans allow parents to open custodial accounts for their children. To open such an account, all your parents need is your birth date and your Social Security number. If you have a bank account, you can link that account to the direct investment plan so you can automatically make optional cash investments to the plan if you choose to do so. The bank account information that your parents will have to supply on the application is as follows:

- The bank account number and type (such as checking or savings account).
- The bank routing number (ABA number). The ABA number and the bank account number are both at the bottom of your check. The branch information can also be found on your check. Ask your bank for these numbers if you are not sure.
- The name of the financial institution.
- The branch address.

STEP #6: KEEPING RECORDS

Throughout this book, we have been emphasizing the importance of keeping records of all your investment transactions, but accurate record keeping is especially important with direct investment plans. With these plans, you can choose to have dividends reinvested in the company's stock but you may have to pay taxes on those dividends depending on how much you receive. This means that you have to keep accurate records of all reinvested dividends. In addition, you must carefully track all the direct investment plan purchases in order to properly calculate the taxes owed when you sell the shares.

PART

4

Having Some Funds

Mutual Funds		
$$$$ ⇒	Recommended Minimum Investment	$1,000 to $3,000
$$ ⇒	Minimum Additional Investment (Optional)	$100 to $300

12

The Goods on Mutual Funds

Not every Teenvestor is comfortable with researching and choosing stocks on their own. Some feel overwhelmed by the massive amounts of financial information produced by companies. Others simply don't have the time to investigate and choose the right stocks for their portfolios. For these Teenvestors, mutual funds may be the perfect investment.

Although mutual funds allow Teenvestors to keep their investment strategy pretty simple without devoting too much time to studying the market, you should still understand what mutual funds are, how they work, and some of the advantages and disadvantages of investing in them.

WHAT IS A MUTUAL FUND?

A *mutual fund*, also known as an *investment company*, is a pool of money that is managed on behalf of investors by a professional fund manager. The fund manager takes the money contributed by the group of mutual fund investors and buys stocks, bonds, and other securities. In return for putting money into the fund, the investors receive shares that represent their portion of the pool of fund investments. Just as you can buy one share of stock, you can also buy a share of a mutual fund. The value of a share of a mutual fund is called its *net asset value (NAV)*. The NAV is reported in daily newspapers or on major financial websites. Box 12.2 gives an example of how the change in NAV can affect your mutual fund investment. In return for managing the fund's investment portfolio, the fund manager charges fees based on the value of the fund's assets. Box 12.3 gives more details of the various people involved in bringing mutual funds to the market.

GENERAL CHARACTERISTICS OF MUTUAL FUNDS

Mutual funds are generally grouped by the types of investments they make:

- *Stock and bond investments.* Some mutual funds invest in stocks, others in bonds, and still others in a combination of stocks and bonds.

- *Domestic/international investments.* Some mutual funds invest mostly in U.S. stocks, while others invest internationally, and some specialize in specific countries.
- *Low-risk/high-risk investments.* Some mutual funds will focus on low-risk investments, while others may invest in much riskier securities.

GENERAL INVESTMENT PHILOSOPHY OF MUTUAL FUNDS

It is also important to understand a fund's investment philosophy and objectives. These objectives will give you a clue as to how risky the fund can be. There are many different types of funds but the major ones are listed below:

- *Money market funds.* Money market funds invest in short-term (less than one year to maturity), high-quality corporate and government bonds. These bonds are very safe investments but, as you probably know, the safer the investment, the less money you stand to make. Thus money market funds are safe but don't earn you

> **BOX 12.3**
> **The Mutual Fund Team**
>
> **Fund Manager:** The mutual fund manager establishes the mutual fund, markets it, and oversees its general administration.
>
> **Portfolio Adviser:** The portfolio adviser is the professional money manager appointed by the mutual fund manager to direct the fund's investments. The fund manager often acts as the portfolio adviser.
>
> **Distributor:** The distributor coordinates the sale of the fund to investors either directly or through a network of authorized dealers.
>
> **Custodian:** The custodian is the bank or trust company appointed by the fund manager to hold all of the securities owned by the fund.
>
> **Transfer Agent and Registrar:** This is the group responsible for maintaining the register of shareholders of the fund.
>
> **Auditor:** The auditor is an independent accountant hired by the fund manager to perform an audit each year and report on the financial statements of the fund.

much in investment returns. The share value of money market funds is pretty stable.

• *Fixed income or bond funds.* Fixed income funds invest in corporate bonds (of various quality), mortgages that pay interest, and preferred stocks that pay regular dividends. The goal of fixed income funds is to provide an investor with a steady stream of interest from the assets in the fund. The share value of fixed income funds will change as interest rates change.

• *Growth funds, equity funds, or stock funds.* These funds invest primarily in stocks of U.S. or foreign companies but may hold other assets as well. The goal is typically to invest in stocks whose value will grow over time. Some growth funds focus on large blue-chip companies, while others invest in smaller or riskier companies. The performance of the fund is affected by the success or failure of specific investments and by the general performance of the stock market.

• *Balanced Funds.* Balanced funds invest in a balanced portfolio of stocks, bonds, and money market instruments (such as short-term U.S. government notes) with the goal of providing reasonable returns with low to moderate risk.

• *Global and foreign funds.* These types of funds may be fixed income, growth, or balanced funds that invest in foreign stocks and bonds. They offer investors international diversification and the chance to indirectly invest in foreign companies. The problem with these funds is that investors face the risks associated with investing in foreign countries (such as the risk of wars in developing countries and the risk of exchange rate changes).

• *Specialty funds.* Specialty funds invest mainly in a specific geographical area (such as Asia) or a specific industry (such as high-tech companies).

• *Index funds.* Index funds invest in a portfolio of securities selected to represent a specific target market index such as the S&P 500. An S&P 500 index fund would invest in the stocks in that index. (See our explanation of popular indices in Chapter 8.)

Despite the variety in the investment philosophy of mutual funds, we recommend that the beginning investor start with stock index funds. You will find more information about index funds in Chapter 13.

HOW MUTUAL FUNDS CAN EARN YOU MONEY

There are three ways in which Teenvestors can make money with mutual funds:

• *Dividends/interest distributions to you.* A fund that invests in stocks will collect dividends from the stocks in the portfolio. Likewise, a fund that invests in bonds will collect interest payments on the bonds. The fund will pass the dividends and interest it receives on to investors who have bought shares in the fund.

• *Sale of the fund's assets by the fund.* If a mutual fund wants to benefit from the increase in value of the stocks or bonds it holds, it sells some of its investments to lock in a profit. This profit is called *capital gains*, and it is passed on to people who own shares in the fund.

• *Sale of your shares.* If a fund does not sell but holds on to the stocks or bonds, the value of its shares (NAV) may increase. A higher NAV reflects the higher value of your investment. If you then sell your shares, you make a profit.

ADVANTAGES OF MUTUAL FUNDS

Mutual funds offer Teenvestors a variety of benefits including:

• *Diversification.* The beauty of mutual funds is that the holdings in a mutual fund are diversified. If you recall from Chapter 8, diversification is the act of investing in several different products (for example, stocks in different industries) so that a decline in the value of one investment does not necessarily affect the value of the other investments in your portfolio. Stock mutual funds hold so many different stocks that a decline in the value of any one stock will not affect the value of the other stocks in the fund. For this reason, many investors see mutual funds as less risky than investing in the stocks of one or two companies. Not all funds are low in risk, however, even if the fund holds several different stocks. A fund that invests in only one sector of the economy, such as Internet-related stocks, which are known to be risky, would be riskier than a fund that invests in multiple industries, such as transportation, banks, and restaurants.

BOX 12.4
Liquidity

Liquidity refers to how easy it is to sell your investments. If you owned a bicycle, for example, and you wanted to sell it because you needed cash right away, you would have a hard time selling it in a short period of time (such as in one day). You would first have to let people know that you are putting the bicycle up for sale, perhaps by putting an ad in your local newspaper and then wait for people to call you to see it. In the investment world, experts would say that a bicycle has low liquidity since it can't be sold immediately when you need the cash. Shares of mutual funds are very liquid because they can be sold in a day since there is always someone ready to purchase them.

• *Professional management.* Mutual funds offer you an opportunity to invest in a product that is professionally managed. Not only are mutual fund managers experienced in investing money but they also have the skills, time, and resources to research different investment opportunities. Thus, mutual funds relieve you of the burden of having to do your own research on different companies in order to decide which company's stock will be a suitable investment. However, you still need to do your homework to determine whether the particular fund that you are interested in is a good investment.

• *Affordability.* With many mutual funds, you can open up an account with a relatively small amount of money. This amount generally ranges from $1,000 to $3,000 for most funds. Some funds will allow you to invest small amounts such as $50 to $100 (to be automatically deducted from your bank account each month) until you meet their minimum required balance.

• *Liquidity.* As an investment, open-end mutual funds are very liquid. They can always be sold back to the fund at a *Net Asset Value* or NAV determined by the fund. See Box 12.4 for more details on liquidity.

111

DISADVANTAGES OF MUTUAL FUNDS

Like any other type of investment, mutual funds have their good points and bad points. We have already discussed the advantages of mutual funds; here are some of their disadvantages:

- *Depending on an investment manager.* When you invest in a mutual fund, you turn your money over to a professional manager. The money you make on your investment depends entirely on the skill of the manager. Even the best money managers are wrong sometimes. Furthermore, it is well known that few managers can consistently do better than the market from year to year. For this reason, investing in index mutual funds takes away the risk of getting a dud for an investment manager.

- *Expenses and commissions.* While many mutual funds allow the investor to invest modest amounts in the fund, this benefit can be overshadowed if the mutual fund imposes hefty fees and other expenses on the investor. On top of the fees and expenses, many mutual funds charge a commission or *sales load*. Since commissions can be as high as 6% to 8%, you need to make sure that you are aware of this expense before investing in any fund. There are three varieties of sales load expenses:

  - *Front-end loads.* Front-end loads are commissions charged by funds when you purchase the fund. When front-end loads are charged, the rate can vary from dealer to dealer and may be negotiable. For example, if you have a 6% front-end load on a share of funds that have a published NAV of $100, you will pay about $106 to buy the share. The NAV of a fund in the papers or your favorite financial website is not necessarily what you will pay for one share of the fund. The NAV does not include the front-end load so you will have to pay more than the NAV to get one share of the mutual fund. The following example is for a hypothetical Teenvestor fund:

Teenvestor Fund NAV = $30, Front = End Load = 5%

$$\frac{\textit{The Cost of One Share of}}{\textit{the Teenvestor Fund}} = \frac{\text{The Fund's NAV}}{1 - \text{Front} = \text{End Load}}$$

$$\frac{30}{1-.05} = \frac{30}{.95} = \$31.58$$

You would pay $31.58 for a share of a Teenvestor fund that has a NAV of $30 and a front-end load of 5%.

- *Back-end loads.* Back-end loads (also called **deferred sales charges**) are sales commissions that you are charged by a fund when you sell your shares (not when you buy them as is the case with front-end load funds). Many back-end loads are charged on a sliding scale that declines for each year that you hold the fund. For example, you might be charged a 5% sales commission if you cash in your fund after a year, 3% if you redeem the fund after three years, and no commission if you redeem the fund after seven years. This sliding scale discourages investors from investing in a fund and moving it quickly to another, more attractive fund a short time later.

- *No loads.* An increasing number of funds are being sold on a no-load basis, in which investors pay no sales charges on either purchase or sale. The obvious advantage with no-load funds is that you can have more of your money working for you. Even with no-load funds, however, the expense ratios can still be high because of management and operating expenses. For this reason, it pays to consider these expenses when looking at investing in no-load funds. For example, you may be happy when mutual funds tell you that they have no *front-end* or *back-end loads* until you discover that they have yearly **12b-1 fees.** 12b-1 fees are marketing/advertising fees you pay for each year you own the mutual fund. If a mutual fund charges 12b-1 fees, they must include it in their *expense ratio.*

Before investing in any mutual fund, make sure you know what fees and commission will be charged by the fund. This is important because the returns quoted by mutual funds don't take into consideration the amount of fees and commissions they charge. In the long run, these expenses may eat into whatever slim gains you may have earned in the mutual fund. Investing in index funds will help you avoid these excessive fees.

THE SAFETY OF MUTUAL FUNDS

When you put your money in a bank, your money is protected by the FDIC (up to a $100,000 limit). With mutual funds, however, there is no such thing as deposit insurance even if you buy your mutual fund from a representative of a bank. While some types of mutual funds are low risk (such as money market funds), others (such as stock funds) can change significantly in price in response to the ups and downs of the economy. The change in the economy can cause the value of your investment to decline, especially over a short period of time. This change in the economic environment that causes the value of your investment to decline is known as market risk (see Chapter 3) and it is a risk you can't totally avoid, though you can lessen its impact by diversifying your investments.

The good news about the risks in mutual funds is that there are special rules and policies to help ensure that the money you invest in them is handled carefully and professionally. These rules include the requirement that an independent auditor reviews and reports on the finances and practices of the funds each year.

WHERE TO GET INFORMATION ABOUT FUNDS

The best source of information about any mutual fund is its ***prospectus***. Here are some important things you should know about prospectuses:

- *Fund details.* A prospectus contains information such as who is managing the fund, the type of investments by mutual funds, its investment philosophy (such as whether it invests in U.S. stocks, U.S. bonds, foreign stocks, and so on), and the various fees and commissions it charges. See some excerpts from a real prospectus in Appendix III.

- *Legal requirements.* Each mutual fund is required by law to file a prospectus with all relevant information before it sells any shares to the public.

- *Simplified documents available.* Prospectuses can be difficult to read so mutual funds usually make available documents that give you the basic information you need without drowning you in legal terms.

13

Buying Your First Mutual Fund, Step by Step

Now that you know some of the basics about mutual funds, let's look at what you need to do to make your very first purchase of a fund. With thousands of funds in the market, it can be just as hard to pick a fund as it is to pick a stock. One good way for you to narrow your investing universe is to stick with index funds. Index funds are mutual funds in which the value follows the value of other stock indexes, such as the S&P 500 index or the Dow Jones Industrial Average. According to data from Morningstar, the leading authority on mutual funds, the returns on index funds beat 70% of the returns on all actively managed funds. Unless you are an investment genius, we recommend you stick to index funds.

You should know, however, that index funds could also lose money since they track the major indices. For example, Box 8.10 in Chapter 8 shows losses in the S&P 500 of 23%, 13%, and 10% in 2002, 2001, and 2000 respectively. If you invested in mutual funds that tracked those indices, you would have lost money for those years. However, if you had

BOX 13.1
Top U.S. Mutual Funds*

1. Vanguard 500 Index
2. PIMCO Total Return Fund
3. Fidelity Magellan
4. American Funds Investment Company of America—A Shares
5. American Funds Washington Mutual Investors Fund—A Shares
6. American Funds Growth Fund of America—A Shares
7. Fidelity Contrafund
8. Fidelity Growth & Income
9. American Funds EuroPacific Growth Fund
10. America Funds New Perspective—A Shares

*Ranked by total assets as of 1/6/03. All are stock funds except for PIMCO, which is a bond fund.

invested in S&P 500 index mutual funds in 1997, 1998, and 1999, you would have had investment profits of about 31%, 27%, and 20%, respectively. This tells you that if you want to invest in mutual funds or stocks, it is better to stay with market index funds or stocks of industry leaders over a long period of time since it is impossible to time the market.

The instructions below can help you start your fund-buying experience with mutual funds that focus their investment strategies on stock indices. To be sure, bond index funds also exist and, once you get the hang of mutual funds, you should probably diversify your portfolio with them. However, for now, we will focus on open-end stock mutual funds.

STEP #1: CHOOSE FROM INDEX FUNDS FOR STARTERS

For your first investment, we recommend that you choose a stock index fund. Please refer to Box 8.12 for a description of the major U.S. stock market indices. The most popular index funds are based on the S&P

500, the NASDAQ, the Wilshire 5000, the Russell 2000, and the Dow. Box 13.3 gives a list of no-load index funds with relatively small minimum balances. Note that just like stocks, mutual funds also have their own symbols. Don't be totally turned off by the $1,000 to $3,000 minimum balance requirements because some funds may allow you to invest smaller amounts if you agree to have a monthly investment amount, such as $100, withdrawn from your bank account until you meet the investment minimum. In addition, if you establish Coverdell Educational Savings or Roth individual retirement accounts (which we will discuss in Chapters 17 and 19), you can invest as little as $250 to $500 in these funds.

Step #2: Get a Copy of the Prospectus

After you have identified a fund that you'd like to invest in, you will need to get a copy of its prospectus for more details on the fund—its investment philosophy, its historical returns, and other characteristics. You can do this in two ways:

- *Go to the company's website.* You can get information directly from the fund's website. For example, we obtained a copy of the Vanguard 500 index fund (symbol VFINX) prospec-

BOX 13.3
No-Load/Low-Balance Index Funds

Fund	Symbol	Index	Minimum Balance for Regular Accounts	Custodial Account Minimum Balance	Phone/Website
Vanguard 500 Index	VFINX	S&P 500	$3,000	$1,000	800-871-3879 www.vanguard.com
USAA S&P 500 Index	USSPX	S&P 500	$3,000	$1,000	800-382-8722 www.usaa.com
Scudder S&P 500 Index	SCPIX	S&P 500	$2,500	$1,000	800-728-3337 www.scudder.com
T. Rowe Price Equity Index 500	PREIX	S&P 500	$2,500	$1,000	800-225-5132 www.troweprice.com
Schwab S&P 500 Fund	SWPIX	S&P 500	$2,500	$1,000	877-488-6762 www.schwab.com
T. Rowe Price Total Equity Market Index	POMIX	Wilshire 5000 Index	$2,500	$1,000	800-225-5132 www.troweprice.com
Vanguard Total Stock Market Index	VTSMX	Wilshire 5000 Index	$3,000	$1,000	800-871-3879 www.vanguard.com
TIAA-CREF Equity Index Fund	TCEIX	Russell 3000 Index	$2,500	$2,500	800-223-1200 www.tiaacref.com
Vanguard Small-Cap Index	NAESX	Russell 2000 Index	$3,000	$1,000	800-871-3879 www.vanguard.com

tus from www.vanguard.com. The company will also mail you a copy of the prospectus if you call them at their toll-free phone numbers.

• *Go to investment websites.* You can also get information about the fund from www.morningstar.com, the most comprehensive mutual fund website on the Internet, which is administered by Morningstar, the mutual fund authority. Other websites where you can get stock information (shown in Box 9.7 of Chapter 9) will also provide you with mutual fund information.

Because big fund companies such as Vanguard and Fidelity have so many funds, you must use the correct mutual fund name or the correct symbol to get the right information. For example, the Vanguard 500 index and the Vanguard Total Market index are different funds with different investment philosophies. Make sure you get the information for the correct fund.

Sometimes the prospectus of a fund will contain information about other funds as well. For example, the prospectus labeled "Vanguard U.S. Stock Index Funds" contains information about the Vanguard 500 index fund as well as the Vanguard Value index fund, the Vanguard Growth index fund, and six other funds.

STEP #3: REVIEW THE PROSPECTUS

We recommend that you read as much of the prospectus as you can. However, if you are short on time, there are four very important sections in most prospectuses

> **BOX 13.4**
> **Teenvestor-Friendly Funds***
>
> Liberty Young Investor Z
> (symbol SRYIX)
> 800-426-3750
> www.libertyfunds.com
>
> USAA First Start Growth
> (symbol UFSGX)
> 800-235-8377
> www.usaa.com
>
> Invesco
> (symbol FLRFX)
> 800-525-8085
> www.invesco.com
>
> American Express
> IDS New Dimensions
> (symbol INDBX)
> 800-437-4332
> www.americanexpress.com
>
> Monetta
> (symbol MLCEX)
> 800-Monetta
> www.monetta.com
>
> *These funds require small minimum balances and small monthly deposits for custodial accounts. In some cases, they produce printed materials to help Teenvestors understand mutual funds. Make sure you check fund performance, philosophy, fees, and expenses before investing. *Do not invest in a fund solely because it has low minimum balance requirements or that it produces good educational materials.*

that we recommend that you read. They are the sections on objectives and strategies, risks, performance, and fees and expenses. Using excerpts of the Vanguard 500 index fund prospectus shown in Appendix III at the end of this book for illustrative purposes only (we are not investment advisers so we can't recommend this fund or any other fund), we will discuss the major sections of the prospectus. While the cover of this prospectus lists a

BOX 13.5
What Funds to Avoid

- Funds with loads
- Fund with annual expense ratios greater than 1%
- Companies with very little experience in managing funds
- Gimmicky funds that focus on narrow investment strategies
- One-hit wonders that have fantastic returns every once in a while—remember these are often the riskiest funds.

group of funds offered by Vanguard, which includes the Vanguard 500 index fund, we are only showing the information related to the Vanguard 500 index fund. For our purposes, we are only interested in the Vanguard 500 index fund investor shares shown in the prospectus.

- *Information from investment objective and strategies*. This section in the prospectuses tells you the fund's philosophy. If the fund you are considering is an index fund, it should refer to that index. For the Vanguard 500 index fund, the prospectus says that the fund looks to track the performance of the S&P 500.

- *Risks*. This is the section in the prospectus that warns you about the risks you may face as an investor in the fund. Read this section carefully so you know what you are buying. For the Vanguard 500 index fund, the risks are that the returns for large-cap stocks may not move in line with the returns from the overall stock market. As a mutual fund index investor, you are probably trying to exactly match the return of the overall market so the prospectus is warning you that the results may deviate from expectations.

- *Performance*. This section shows the return on the fund. It often shows a comparison of the fund's return to some market benchmark. In the case of the Vanguard 500 index fund, the fund's yearly

BOX 13.6
The Vanguard 500 Index Annual Total Returns*
(Investor Shares)

	PAST ONE-YEAR	PAST FIVE-YEAR	PAST TEN-YEAR
The Vanguard 500 Index Fund	−12.02%	10.66%	12.84%
S&P 500	−11.89%	10.70%	12.94%

*Before-tax returns as of 12/31/01

return is shown as well as one-year, five-year, and ten-year returns, which are compared to the S&P 500 returns. Box 13.6 compares the Vanguard 500 index fund's performance to that of the S&P 500. As you can see, the two returns are pretty close and, therefore, the fund's objective is achieved. You can also see that 2001 was a bad year for the S&P 500 and for the Vanguard 500 index fund.

• *Fees.* This is a very important section, especially when it comes to index funds. The fee table below for the Vanguard 500 index fund shows that the fund has no front-end load, although there is an account maintenance fee of $10 per year if you are holding a

BOX 13.7
The Vanguard 500 Index Fund Fees
(Investor Shares)

	FEES
Sales Charge (front-end load)	None
Deferred Sales Charge	None
Annual Account Maintenance Fee (for fund balances under $10,000)	$10

BOX 13.8
The Vanguard 500 Index Fund Annual Expenses
(Investor Shares)

	EXPENSES
Management Expenses	.16%
Distribution & Service (12b-1) fee	None
Other Expenses	.02%
Total Annual Fund Operating Expenses	.18%

mutual fund balance of less than $10,000. Box 13.7 shows a summary of the fees for the fund.

• *Expenses.* Expenses are paid annually from the fund's assets. Ideally, operating expenses should be less than 1% of the investment amount. The yearly operating expense ratio as shown in Box 13.8 is .18%—pretty low in our books. An expense ratio less than 1% is a good thing.

STEP #4: BUYING A FUND

If you have decided to buy an index fund, there are two ways for you to purchase the fund:

• *Buy directly from the fund.* You can buy funds directly from big fund companies like Vanguard and Fidelity without going through a broker. As long as you meet the fund's minimum purchase requirements, you can buy as many shares of the fund as you'd like at the stated NAV. The advantage here is that you don't have to pay any additional fees to a broker. For Teenvestors who wish to buy one index fund from only one fund company, this is the best and cheapest alternative available. To buy the fund directly from the company, call them for an application, mail it in with the required minimum balance, and you are all set.

• *Buy through a broker.* If, on the other hand, you want to buy a mixture of funds from different companies such as Vanguard, Fidelity, Schwab, and T. Rowe Price, it probably makes sense to use a broker. With an online broker, once you fill out an application to buy and sell stocks and funds, you can buy any variety of stocks and mutual funds you want. By contrast, if you want to buy a variety of funds directly from different companies, you will have to fill out an application for each company, and this can be a pain in the neck. The disadvantage with a broker is that the convenience of having a smorgasbord of funds to choose from will cost you. In addition, not all deep-discount online brokers offer a wide selection of funds to choose from. If you want to be able to buy both stocks and mutual funds from an online broker, make sure to ask whether you can do so before signing up with the broker. (Refer to our list of affordable online brokers in Box 9.11 in Chapter 9.)

STEP #5: BUY PERIODICALLY

For index funds, we suggest that you use the dollar-cost averaging method of stock purchases (see Chapter 9). With this method, you invest the same dollar amount in buying stocks or mutual funds each month (or in other periods such as every two months), thus avoiding the risk with trying to time the market.

STEP #6: KEEP GOOD RECORDS

Keep all records that you get from your broker or from the mutual fund company. As taxes are a bit trickier with mutual funds than with stocks, you must be particularly careful to keep every scrap of paper you get from your mutual fund company that records all your transactions.

14

Exchange Traded Funds

Exchange traded funds (ETFs) are investments that have characteristics of both stocks and mutual funds. To review for a moment, a stock is an ownership interest in a company. It is traded on an exchange, and the price can change from minute to minute. By contrast, a mutual fund share is an ownership interest in a diversified basket of stocks, and the price (or NAV) of one share of the fund (at least for open-end funds) is generally calculated once a day. To sell or buy mutual funds, you'd generally have to wait until 4 P.M. on the day of your transaction to get the value of the shares you are selling or buying.

Another difference between stocks and mutual funds, as far as Teen-vestors are concerned, is that it takes a lot more money to invest in mutual funds than in stocks. As we explained in Chapter 13, the minimum balance for the listed no-load index funds is generally about $3,000. While it's true that custodial, retirement, and educational savings accounts can have minimum balance limits as low as $1,000, or less, this is still a lot of money for

127

BOX 14.1
Websites for ETF Educational Information

American Stock Exchange
www.amex.com

Barklays Global Investors
www.ishares.com

Nuveen Investments
www.etfconnect.com

NASDAQ
www.nasdaq.com

Morningstar
www.morningstar.com

State Street Global Advisors
www.streettracks.com

young or first-time investors. Stocks, on the other hand, can be purchased for about the price quoted when you trade, without any minimum purchase requirements.

DEFINING AN ETF

ETFs, also called *index shares*, are investments that represent a diversified group of companies (just like mutual funds) but trade like stocks. They've been around since about 1993, which is a short time for an investment product. At the time of this writing, there were close to 120 stock-based ETFs in the market and just a handful of bond-based ETFs. Check our website, www.teenvestor.com/etf.htm for developments in index stocks and bonds.

ETFS AND THE SMALL INVESTOR

One of the great things about ETFs is that Teenvestors don't need thousands of dollars to buy into them unlike many mutual funds. Box 14.3 shows the most popular ETFs at the time of this writing and their prices per share.

There are numerous other advantages to owning ETFs besides their accessibility to Teenvestors. They also have very low expenses (even lower than mutual funds) and they are better, taxwise, for Teenvestors. Box 14.5 compares stocks, open-end mutual funds, and ETFs.

BOX 14.2
Broad-Market ETFs

ETF	Index Tracked	Symbol	Expense Ratio in %	Website
Standard & Poor's Depository Receipts or SPDRS* (Also known as "Spiders")	S&P 500	SPY	.12	www.spdrindex.com
ishares S&P 500 Index Fund	S&P 500	IVV	.09	www.ishares.com
Vanguard's Total Stock Market VIPERs Index	Wilshire 5000	VTI	.15	www.vanguard.com
The Dow Industrials Diamonds	The Dow	DIA	.18	www.djindexes.com
streetTRACKS Dow Jones U.S. Large-Cap Value	The Dow Jones Large-Cap Value Index	ELV	.20	www.streettracks.com
Standard & Poor's Mid-Cap 400 Depository Receipts	S&P Mid-Cap 400 Index	MDY	.25	www.spdrindex.com
ishares Russell 2000 Value Index Fund	Russell 2000 Index	IWN	.25	www.ishares.com
ishares Russell Mid-Cap Index Fund	Russell Mid-Cap Index	IWR	.20	www.ishares.com
NASDAQ -100 Index Tracking Stock (Also known as "Qubes")	NASDAQ 100 Index	QQQ	.20	www.nasdaq.com

*The first ETF introduced in January 1993 by a subsidiary of the AMEX

BOX 14.3
Heavily Traded ETFs*

ETF	Symbol	Value per Share ($)*
NASDAQ-100 Index Tracking Stock	QQQ	24.37
SPDRS	SPY	88.23
DIAMONDS	DIA	83.51
Mid-Cap SPDRS	MDY	78.65
ishares Russell 3000	IWV	48.96
Vanguard Total Stock VIPERs	VTI	82.63

*As of 12/31/02

BOX 14.4
Advantages of ETFs

- They are a good way to hold diversified stocks without having to diversify on your own.
- They generally charge lower annual expense ratios than mutual funds.
- They have lower capital gains taxes as the fund does not do much trading so capital gains are minimal.
- They have all-day tracking and trading.
- Their initial investment amount can be less than $100 as opposed to an index mutual fund investment minimum that's generally around $2,500.

BOX 14.5

Comparison of Stocks, No-Load Mutual Funds, and ETFs

	When the Price Is Set for Buying and Selling	Minimum Investment Balance	Fees	Yearly Expenses	Tax Consequences
Stock	Price changes continuously during the trading day	The cost of the stock	Brokerage fees for buying the stock plus whatever fees are charged for falling below the account's minimum balances or for infrequent trading	None	You'll get dividends so you'll owe taxes on those dividends
No-Load Open-Ended Mutual Funds	The NAV (approximately, the buying and selling price) is typically set after 4 P.M. on the day you want to buy or sell; your transaction is made at that time	Typically $1,000 to $3,000 for popular index funds	Whatever fees are charged for falling below the fund's minimum balances	Ranges from .18% to .40% for no-load funds shown in Box 13.3	You'll get dividends so you'll owe taxes on those dividends
ETF	Price changes continually during the trading day	The cost of the ETF—the most popular ETFs cost less than $100	Brokerage fees for buying the stock plus whatever fees are charged for falling below the account's minimum balances or for infrequent trading	Ranges from .09% to .25% for broad-market ETFs shown in Box 14.2	You'll get dividends and very little in capital gains so you'll owe taxes on the dividends and the miniscule capital gains

BUYING ETFS

Buying ETFs is as easy as buying stocks from your online broker. The only difference is that with ETFs, there is a prospectus available to help you understand the fund's investment strategy. You should make absolutely sure that you are investing in the ETF of the index you'd like to hold, such as the S&P 500 or the Dow. Any of the websites that can give you a stock quote can provide you with the information you need about your ETF of choice. Our first stop is usually the Morningstar investment website, www.morningstar.com, but you can try the other research websites we list in Box 9.7 in Chapter 9. Type in the symbol for the ETF you are interested in researching and you will get information on the fund's profile. Alternatively, you can go directly to the websites of the company offering the ETF, as shown in Box 14.2, for basic information and prospectuses.

PART
5

Money for Reading, 'Riting, and 'Rithmetic

College Savings Plans (529 Plans)		
$$ ⇒ Recommended Minimum Investment	$100 to $300	
$ ⇒ Minimum Additional Investment (Optional)	$30 to $100	

15

Money for College

Information about investing for college is one of the most frequently accessed sections on our website, Teenvestor.com. Your parents may already be aware of some of the options available to them when it comes to planning for your college costs. This chapter can help you and your parents begin an investment plan that can be used to meet higher education expenses. Since you can't invest on your own anyway without a custodial account and since college savings can have an impact on your parents' ability to receive financial aid for your college education, your parents have to be more involved in the college investments discussed in this chapter than with other investments we've discussed so far.

Typically, parents are the ones paying for their children's college education. However, with ever-rising college costs, college-bound students are also chipping in. Although it's highly unlikely that you, as a Teenvestor, will be able to invest enough money to pay for your college education, by using the investment options discussed in this chapter, you can save for your college books, supplies, and equipment while providing your parents with welcome tax benefits associated with these investments. For example, these investments are a great way for Teenvestors to save for a laptop computer.

A good investment to consider when saving for college is a *college savings plan*, also known as a *529 plan*. These are state-run investment plans that are used for paying for college. Nearly all states have their own version of a college savings plan where as little as $5 can be invested in a tax-advantaged fund sponsored by that state. We recommend initial investments of at least $100 to $300, however, because of the fees that you may be charged for opening an account.

HOW COLLEGE SAVINGS PLANS WORK

College savings plans exist to encourage parents, Teenvestors, and others to prepare for the college expenses they may face in the future. There are usually two types of plans: prepaid college plans and college investment plans.

Prepaid College Plans

With prepaid college plans, you are required to make deposits into a state-sponsored account for a number of years to cover anticipated college costs at a public higher-education institution. As a Teenvestor, you probably will not be able to make the required payments to prepaid college plans. Your parents, however, may find the following details about these types of plans valuable if they hope to prepay your college tuition at a state school:

BOX 15.2
Types of College Savings Plans (529 Plans)

Prepaid College Plans—The account owner is required to make specific deposits in order to guarantee (or nearly guarantee) that college expenses in state institutions will be met for the college-bound beneficiary.

College Investment Plans—The investment options chosen by the account owner can be changed as the college-bound beneficiary approaches college age. There is virtually no guarantee of minimum returns on investments.

- *Guaranteed funds.* The money you deposit in these plans is guaranteed (or nearly guaranteed), which means that you can attend any public college in your state without requiring additional payments by you or your parents—even if tuition increases. In many of these prepaid college plans, you have no choice in terms of how your money will be invested by the state.

- *Shortfalls made up.* In a few of these prepaid college plans, the state makes up any shortfall in the amount of money you will have to pay in a state college if college costs have gone up more than anticipated.

- *Payments based on tuition projections.* In the prepaid college plans, the payments are based on the state's best guess of what college will cost when you're ready to attend. When you are ready for college, you can attend any public college in the state. For example, Alabama's prepaid college plan, called the Prepaid Affordable College Tuition Program or PACT, covers the cost of four years of undergraduate college education for any public college or university in Alabama. If the beneficiary of the PACT account goes to an institution outside of Alabama, the state pays the average tuition and mandatory fees at the public four-year colleges in Alabama to the institution.

College Investment Plans

In many college investment plans, you have a choice as to how your money is invested but there are no guarantees about the amount of money your investments will make or about the tuition payments to a public institution in your state. However, college investment plans can be great for Teenvestors because you can invest as little or as much as you want in order to save for college. Some of the features common to these plans are:

- *Age-Based Plans.* While each state has its own investment options, these options can change as the person for whom the plan was started gets closer to college age. Such plans whose composition can change with age are called *age-based plans*.

- *Funds are moved around.* In some state college investment plans, your investments are automatically moved from aggressive (risky) portfolios to more conservative portfolios, depending on your age when the plan is established. In these plans, as the young person approaches college age, the money in the plan is moved into more conservative investments. For example, a Teenvestor who opens a college investment plan at age 14 will only have about three years before he needs the money for school. Given this short time period, he should put money into conservative college investment plans that invest only in low-risk investment such as Certificates of Deposit or money markets. Meanwhile, a parent who has a one-year-old child will not need the college savings for another 17 years or so, when the child will be ready for college. This means that the parent can afford to put money in more aggressive (and hence, more risky) investment options such as stocks.

THE ROLE STATES PLAY IN COLLEGE SAVINGS PLANS

State governments run college savings plans, but the investments are managed by private organizations. For example, the investments in New York's college savings plan are managed by TIAA, a part of TIAA-CREF, a leading financial services organization.

Each state has a different name for its college savings plan. Kentucky's college savings plan is called the Kentucky Education Savings Plan Trust, while Hawaii's is called TuitionEdge. Sometimes a state may have one name for its prepaid college plan and another for its college investment plan. Maryland calls its prepaid college plan the Maryland Prepaid College Trust and its college investment plan, the Maryland College Investment Plan.

As long as a plan comes under the IRS's 529 plan designation, you are looking at a college savings plan no matter what the state calls it.

OPENING AN ACCOUNT

Anyone can open an account—Teenvestors, parents, grandparents, uncles, aunts, and friends. Theoretically, a total stranger can open an account for you.

When an account is opened, the person who opens it, otherwise known as the *account owner*, has to designate whom should benefit from the account. A Teenvestor can designate herself as the person who will benefit from the account.

The person for whom the account is opened is called the *beneficiary*. Anyone with a Social Security number can be a beneficiary, but each account may have only one designated beneficiary. There are no restrictions based on age, relationship to the account owner, or, in some cases, state residency of the account owner or the beneficiary. As long as a Teenvestor has a Social Security number, she can designate herself as the beneficiary. Multiple accounts can be set up for the same beneficiary as long as the plan's maximum limit is not exceeded.

At the time of this writing, the Arkansas Gift College Investment Plan had a maximum contribution limit of $245,000 for any one individual. In Pennsylvania's plan, called the Tuition Account Program (TAP), the aggregate maximum contribution currently allowed is $260,000. These maximum amounts will probably never be reached by a Teenvestor, but if your parents are the ones who have set up the account, they should know about these limits since it could affect their contribution limit if they intend to put a lot of money into the account for your college education.

ACCOUNT WITHDRAWALS

You can only take money out of a college savings plan account without a penalty if the money is to be used to pay for what's called *qualified withdrawals*. Qualified withdrawals are withdrawals that are to be used to pay for: tuition, fees, textbooks, supplies, equipment, and other expenses in an *eligible educational institution*.

Eligible educational institutions are as follows: colleges, universities, vocational schools, or postsecondary educational institutions that can participate in a student aid program administered by the U.S. Department of Education. When in doubt as to whether a school is considered an eligible educational institution, just ask the educational institution if it qualifies as one.

An *unqualified withdrawal* occurs when the account owner takes money out of the account for purposes other than higher education. If the account owner makes an unqualified withdrawal, he will have to pay a 10% penalty on the earnings in the account as well as federal and (probably) state income tax.

WHY COLLEGE SAVINGS PLANS ARE SO GREAT

There are many advantages to college savings plans:

BOX 15.4
Advantages Of College Savings Plans

- No federal tax paid on earnings.
- High income limitations means that if your income is high, you are still allowed to invest
- Your money is professionally managed.
- There are low minimum investments.

- *No federal taxes.* Neither you nor your parents will pay federal taxes on the earnings on a college savings plan as long as you use it for qualified higher education expenses. In addition, in many states, no state taxes are owed.

- *Guarantees.* In some cases, coverage of your college costs are guaranteed.

- *No income limitations.* Unlike the Coverdell Educational Savings Account—another tax-advantaged savings account that we'll discuss in Chapter 17—individuals at any income level can contribute to the plan. This means that if your parents make a lot of money, they can still open a college savings plan account for you.

- *Professional money management.* You have professional money managers such as TIAA-CREF, Fidelity, and others investing your money for you.

- *Low minimum investments.* The minimum investment requirements are low—as low as $5—and you can invest as much as a few hundred thousand dollars in total.

THE DISADVANTAGES OF COLLEGE SAVINGS PLANS

Since January 1, 2002, college savings plans have become more attractive to adults who want to save for their children's (or relatives') educations. As we mentioned earlier, the biggest change in these plans is that there are no federal taxes due on the gains earned in them as long as the money is used for certain educational expenses. But there are a few catches to these plans that young investors (and their parents) should be aware of:

- *States run their own plans.* Because the states run their own plans, they can set their own rules about the withdrawal of the money, they can change where they invest your money, they can change the fees they charge associated with participation in the plan, they can determine whether contributions to the plan are deductible from state taxes, or they can impose any other conditions on the accounts. Each plan has its own participation terms, and these terms can vary considerably from state to state.

- *Fees.* Some plans are expensive because they charge you a sales fee, a yearly maintenance fee, and a fee that goes to the investment managers (such as TIAA-CREF). For this reason, we strongly recommend that, before selecting a particular plan, you make sure you understand the fees that are associated with the plan. Watch out for sales load and annual expense ratios. You can avoid some of these excessive charges by investing in low-cost and low-risk college savings plans such as the ones we discuss in the next chapter.

- *Investment choices are limited.* In the plans with guaranteed returns, you can't decide exactly how your money will be invested. In the age-based plans, you have slightly more flexibility in investment choices but you are still bound by preestablished investment guidelines.

- *Some plans have terrible track records.* Unfortunately, the track record of some college savings plans is terrible. True, many of these plans have been around for only three years so they haven't had a chance to recover from recent market downturns. However, this doesn't make it easier to swallow losses of 15% or more in some plans, which is worse than the S&P 500 loss of about 12% in 2001—one of the worst years for the market after the ten-year boom that ended in 2000. As a Teenvestor starting to invest just a few years before going to college, you don't have time to wait for the plan to recover from huge losses. This is why doing your research before investing is particularly important when investing for college.

• *You can't move your money around as often as you might like.* You can only move your money to a different plan once a year. So if you happen to invest in a dog of a plan, you are stuck for a whole year even while the value of your college savings are going down.

• *State tax exemption not assured.* If you are investing in an out-of-state plan, you may not be exempt from state taxes (which some states offer on the earnings of the plan). Get all the facts before you invest in another state's college savings plan. Find out what disadvantage you may have as an out-of-state investor.

• *Possible expiration of tax benefits.* The current federal tax benefits associated with college savings plans—especially the benefit that cancelled federal taxes on earnings on these plans—will expire unless reaffirmed by Congress in 2010. In other words, if the tax benefits are not reaffirmed, taxes will be due on the earnings when money is pulled out of the account to meet educational expenses.

FREQUENTLY ASKED QUESTIONS

Lots of questions come up when discussing college savings plans. In this section, we respond to the most common questions visitors to our website, www.teenvestor.com, frequently ask us about these plans.

Can a Minor Open an Account?

Like all of the investments discussed in this book, if you are a minor, you are not allowed to open an account on your own. An adult will have to open a custodial account for you (see Box 4.1 in Chapter 4). Once you are considered an adult under the law (in most states, when you've reached 18 years of age), the money in the account becomes yours to use for your qualified educational expenses.

If I Open a College Savings Plan, Will I Still Be Eligible for Financial Aid?

Your eligibility for financial aid will depend on your family's financial situation at the time you enroll in college. While each college uses its own formula, you can expect about 6% of your parents' assets (and 35% of your assets) to be considered in the formula for determining financial aid eligibility. According to the U.S. Department of Education, the money in college saving plans may be considered an asset of the account owner. In other words, when determining whether you are eligible for financial aid, the amount in your college savings plan becomes part of the pool of assets that colleges will expect to be used to finance your college education. This, of course, could lower your parents' ability to receive financial aid. However, if your parents' yearly income is over $50,000, they probably won't get financial aid and, thus, college savings plans can help you and your parents invest for college.

Are My Investments Guaranteed?

Some college savings plans have minimum return levels. For example, one of the investment choices, the guaranteed option, offered by California's ScholarShare Program, provides a guarantee of principal and a fixed rate of return. The vast majority of college savings plans, however, make no such guarantees. There is no evidence that guaranteed funds perform better or worse than nonguaranteed funds. However, the protection of your contributions to the plan or the guarantee of a fixed rate of return no doubt is very attractive to those who do not want to lose any money by participating in a college savings plan. These types of plans become particularly attractive when the stock market is not doing well.

Do I Have a Choice as to How the Money Is Invested?

In some instances, you do have a limited choice in determining the investment mix of the plan. For example, California's ScholarShare Program gives you five investment choices for your contributions. Generally choices in college savings plans range from conservative portfolios (mostly bonds) to aggressive portfolios (mostly growth stocks).

Am I Limited to Schools in My State?

All the plans allow you to use the money accumulated in your plan to meet the expenses of any accredited college, public or private, in the United States and in some foreign countries. So, if you change your mind about what college to attend, the money in your college savings plan is still available for use in another school.

What Happens If I Don't Go to College?

If you are just delaying college, you can keep the money in the plan until a later date when you are ready for college. Or, if you don't go to college, you can transfer the account to another family member who is college bound.

Can I Open More Than One Account?

Yes. As long as the total amount of the account does not exceed the maximum amount allowed by your state for any one beneficiary. As a Teenvestor, we doubt you will ever exceed such limits.

16

Choosing a College Savings Plan, Step by Step

STEP #1: DECIDE IF A COLLEGE SAVINGS PLAN IS RIGHT FOR YOU

The decision whether to invest in a college savings plan probably depends on your prospects for getting financial aid when you are ready to go to college. For this reason, your parents have to be fully involved in any college savings plan considerations. Here are three things you should know about college savings plans and financial aid.

• *College savings plans are great for high-income families.* College savings plans work well for families who make a lot of money and are sure they won't qualify for financial aid. Talk to

147

BOX 16.2
Financial Aid and College Savings Plans

Financial aid offices in colleges are now struggling with how to treat money in college savings plans—whether as assets of the parents or assets of the college-bound beneficiary. We know that technically the assets belong to the parents and, so far, public colleges, using Federal Aid formulas, have been treating them as such and assessing only 5.6% when figuring out how much parents should contribute to their children's education. Public colleges assess 35% of the student's assets when deciding how much students should contribute to their own education.

We think that ultimately, however, colleges may end up assessing the assets in these accounts more than the 5.6% charge as a way of reducing the amount expended by colleges on student aid. New rules governing financial aid that are expected to be written by Congress for the 2004–2005 academic year will probably clarify the assessment figures.

Even though the money initially invested in a college savings plan is currently treated as a parental asset by public colleges, when the money is withdrawn, colleges expect that 50% of the earnings (the gains) in the account will go toward financing your education. For this reason, colleges will reduce the amount of aid that you may have otherwise received. However, the flip side of this is that since most of that aid would have been in the form of loans anyway, by investing in a college savings plan over a long period of time, which makes lots of gains, you can significantly reduce the amount of student loans that you have to take out to finance your education.

---

your parents to see if they think they can qualify for financial aid when you reach college age. The websites in Box 16.3 can help them tell if you are likely to qualify for financial aid when you are ready for college. If you won't qualify for financial aid, your parents would probably want to take advantage of the substantial tax advantages provided to those who invest in college savings plans.

• *College savings plans are not so good for families who don't make as much money.* In general, if your family's income is less than $50,000, you may qualify for financial aid. If you qualify for financial aid when it is time to go to college, the amount of money in your college savings plan would probably reduce the amount of financial aid you would receive from the college you plan to attend.

• *Financial aid is mostly loans.* Keep in mind, however, that most financial aid is in the form of student loans even for those who do not make much money. It's likely that a very significant portion of your financial aid package will consist of student loans. For this reason, many parents find it useful to consult with a financial adviser for the best course of action. In addition, the websites listed in Box 16.3 can help you and your parents gain a better understanding of how financial aid works. This will help determine whether your family will qualify for financial aid and, if so, whether it's a good idea for you to invest in a college savings plan.

STEP #2: BEGIN WITH YOUR STATE'S PLAN

If you or your parents decide to invest in a college savings plan or 529 plan, we recommend that you start with your own state's plan. (See Box 16.7 at the end of this chapter for a list of all state plans.) We recommend that you keep the following things in mind about state plans:

• *State income tax benefits.* A majority of the states offer tax benefits to residents who contribute to their state's college savings plans. If you live in a high-tax state, your parents may find a college savings plan particularly attractive, since tax benefits can be significant.

• *Plans are constantly being updated.* Plans are constantly being updated, but you can keep up with them by reading the special articles appearing in the websites and publications listed in Box 16.4. *Kiplinger's, SmartMoney, USA Today,* and other publications carry lots of articles about college savings plans.

You can also get the printed plan material through the websites or you can have them mailed to you. The college savings plans for each state usually originates from the State Treasurer. If you want to find your State Treasurer's website, go to the website of the National Association of State Treasurers at www.nast.net. Go to www.teenvestor.com/college-plans.htm for links to the plans for each state.

STEP #3: CONSIDER THE STRESS-FREE OPTIONS

If you don't want to fret too much about which college savings plans to invest in, consider some of the simple no-load (for example, no sales charge) investment choices out there involving Certificates of Deposit and index funds. These plans are relatively less risky and some have guaranteed returns. Plans are always changing, but Box 16.6 shows some of the simplest no-load plans.

STEP #4: STUDY THE PLAN MATERIAL

You should evaluate a college savings plan the same way you'd investigate mutual funds. After all, the investment choices in a college savings plan (especially those that give you the flexibility to move your money around to different investment categories) is similar to an investment in mutual funds. We strongly recommend that your parents stay involved in any decisions you make about a college savings plan option. When you receive the plan documents from your state or the state's investment manager, here are the things you should pay particular attention to:

- *Fees.* Find out the yearly expense ratio for your choice of college savings plans. Because some of these plans are actually managed by fund companies like Vanguard and Fidelity and some are sold through brokers, they will charge various levels of expenses and sales loads. For example, one of the three college investment plans offered by Arizona (managed by Securities Management and Research) charges a sales load of up to 5% and an expense ratio that generally ranges from 1.25% to an incredible 14.71%—heavy penalties for the privilege of investing in this specific plan. You should be able to find college savings plans that have no sales load charges and that have expense ratios around 1%, such as the plans managed by Vanguard. See the choices shown in Box 16.6 for a start. Once again, plan features are constantly changing so keep up by reading current articles on college savings plans or check our website, www.teenvestor.com/collegeplans.htm.

- *Returns.* Returns (for example, the profit you make) in the various funds offered by college savings plans are important, but you

BOX 16.6
Relatively Simple & Safe No-Load Plans*
(Open to Out-Of-State Investors)

State	Investment	Investment Details	Annual Expenses (% of Assets)
Alaska www.uacollegesavings.com	T. Rowe Price Stock & Bond Funds	You choose from an array of funds with various risk levels	.32 to 1.06
Arizona arizona.collegesavings.com	CollegeSure CD	Minimum return of 4%—linked to increase in average college cost	None
Iowa www.collegesavingsiowa.com	Vanguard Stock & Bond Index Funds	You choose from an array of funds with various risk levels	.28 to .30
Montana montana.collegesavings.com	CollegeSure CD	Minimum return of 4%—linked to increase in average college cost	None
New Mexico www.tepnm.com	State Street Global Advisors Bond Fund	Bonds with medium maturities—some risky bonds included	.79
Utah www.uesp.org	Vanguard 500 Index and other Vanguard Stock & Bond Index Funds	You choose from an array of funds with various risk levels	.28 to .30
Ten States with Plans Administered by TIAA-CREF www.tiaacref.org	Guaranteed Options from TIAA-CREF	Minimum return is 3%—more possible	None

*See www.teenvestor.com/collegeplans.htm for updates/amendments

must compare the returns to those of other funds in the same time period. In a bad economy, nearly all funds perform poorly. Once again, if you are concerned about the risk in portfolios, consider the guaranteed prepaid tuition options offered by various states and relatively low-risk options offered by some of the plans in existence.

BOX 16.7
College Savings Plans by State

State	College Savings Plan	Phone Number	Website[1]
Alabama	Prepaid Affordable College Tuition Program (PACT)	800-252-7228	www.treasury.state.al.us
	Alabama Higher Education 529 Fund	866-529-2228	www.vankampen.com/products/529
Alaska	Advanced College Tuition Program (ACT)	866-277-1005	www.uacollegesavings.com
Arizona[2]	Arizona Family College Savings Program	602-258-2435 888-667-3239 800-888-2723 888-923-3355	www.acpe.asu.edu www.smrinvest.com www.waddell.com arizona.collegesavings.com
Arkansas	Gift College Investing Plan	877-442-6553	www.thegiftplan.com
California	Golden State ScholarShare	877-728-4338	www.scholarshare.com
Colorado	CollegeInvest Prepaid Tuition Plan	800-478-5651	www.collegeinvest.org
	Scholars Choice	888-572-4652	www.scholars-choice.com
Connecticut	Connecticut Higher Education Trust (CHET)	888-799-2438	www.state.ct.us/ott www.aboutchet.com
Delaware	Delaware College Investment Plan	800-544-1655	www.state.de.us/treasure/college.html
	Unique College Investment Plan	800-544-1722	
	U.Fund College Investment Plan	800-544-2776	
Florida	Florida Prepaid College Program	800-552-4723	www.fsba.state.fl.us/prepaid
Georgia	The Georgia Higher Education Savings Plan	877-424-4377	www.gacollegesavings.com

(continued)

State	College Savings Plan	Phone Number	Website[1]
Hawaii	TuitionEdge	866-529-3343	www.tuitionedge.com
Idaho	Idaho College Savings Program	866-433-2533	www.idsaves.org
Illinois	College Illinois	877-877-3724	www.collegeillinois.com
	Bright Start	877-432-7444	www.brightstart savings.com
Indiana	The College Choice 529 Investment Plan	866-400-7526	www.college choiceplan.com
Iowa	College Savings Iowa	888-672-9116	www.college savingsiowa.com
Kansas	Learning Quest Education Savings Program	800-579-2203	www.learningquest savings.com
Kentucky	Kentucky Education Savings Plan Trust	877-598-7878	www.kentuckytrust.org
Louisiana	Louisiana Student Tuition Assistance and Revenue Trust (START)	800-259-5626, extension 1012	www.treasury.state.la.us
Maine	NextGen College Investing Plan	877-463-9843	www.nextgenplan.com
Maryland	Maryland Prepaid College Trust	888-463-4723	www.college savingsmd.org
	Maryland College Investment Plan		
Massachusetts	Massachusetts U. Plan	800-449-6332	www.mefa.org
	Massachusetts U. Fund		
Michigan	Michigan Education Savings Program	877-861-6377	www.misaves.com
	Michigan Education Trust (MET)	800-MET-4-KID	www.michigan.gov/ treasury (look under "Education")

(continued)

Choosing a College Savings Plan, Step by Step

State	College Savings Plan	Phone Number	Website[1]
Minnesota	Minnesota College Savings Plan	877-338-4646	www.mnsaves.org
Mississippi	The Mississippi Prepaid Affordable College Tuition Program (MPACT)	800-987-4450	www.treasury.state.ms.us/mpact.htm
	Mississippi Affordable College Savings Program (MACS)	601-359-5255	www.college savingsms.com
Missouri	Missouri Saving for Tuition Program (MOST)	888-414-6678	www.missourimost.org
Montana	Montana Family Education Savings Program	800-888-2723	montana.college savings.com
Nebraska	College Savings Plan of Nebraska	888-993-3746	www.planfor collegenow.com
Nevada	America's College Savings Plan	877-529-5295	www.nevada treasurer.com
New Hampshire	The UNIQUE College Investing Plan	800-544-1722	www.state.nh.us/treasury
New Jersey	New Jersey Better Education Savings Trust (NJBEST)	877-465-2378	www.hesaa.org/students/njbest
New Mexico	The Education Plan of New Mexico	800-499-7581	www.tepnm.com
New York	New York's College Savings Program	877-697-2837	www.nysaves.org
North Carolina	National College Savings Program	866-866-2362	www.treasurer.state.nc.us www.cfnc.org
North Dakota	College Save	866-728-3529	www.collegesave 4u.com
Ohio	CollegeAdvantage	800-233-6734	www.college advantage.com

(continued)

State	College Savings Plan	Phone Number	Website[1]
Oklahoma	Oklahoma College Savings Plan	877-654-7284	www.ok4saving.org
Oregon	Oregon College Savings Plan	866-772-8464	www.oregoncollege savings.com
Pennsylvania	Pennsylvania Tuition Account Program	800-440-4000	www.patap.org
Rhode Island	CollegeBoundfund	888-324-5057	www.collegebound fund.com
South Carolina	South Carolina Tuition Prepayment Program (SCTPP)	888-772-4723	www.scgrad.org
South Dakota	South Dakota's College Access 529 Plan	866-529-7462	www.college access529.com
Tennessee	Tennessee's Baccalaureate Education System Trust (BEST) Prepaid Tuition Plan	888-486-2378	www.tnbest.org
	Baccalaureate Education System Trust (BEST) Savings Plan		
Texas	Texas Tomorrow Fund	800-445-4723	www.texastomorrow fund.org
Utah	Utah Educational Savings Plan Trust (UESP)	800-418-2551	www.uesp.org
Vermont	The Vermont Higher Education Investment Plan (VHEIP)	800-637-5860	www.vsac.org
Virginia	Virginia Education Savings Trust (VEST)	888-567-0540	www.virginia529.com
	Virginia Prepaid Education Program (VPEP)		
	CollegeAmerica		

(continued)

State	College Savings Plan	Phone Number	Website[1]
Washington	Guaranteed Education Tuition (GET)	877-438-8848	www.get.wa.gov
West Virginia	Smart529, The College Savings Solution	866-574-3542	www.smart529.com
Wisconsin	EdVest	888-338-3789	www.edvest.com
Wyoming	College Achievement Plan	877-529-2655	www.college achievementplan.com

1. Wherever we could, we have given you the website of the State Treasurer (which is typically responsible for college savings plans) and the website for the specific plan options. The treasurer's website is important because it should alert you to all changes or expansion of the state's current college savings plans.

2. Arizona has three types of college savings plans that can be bought from different companies. The most basic college savings plan Arizona has is the CollegeSure CDs offered by the College Savings Bank. These CDs guarantee a minimum return and charges no load or expenses. The other college savings plan choices in Arizona are mutual funds with relatively expensive sales loads and expense ratios. This Arizona plan is a good illustration as to how a state can have several plans with various levels of attractiveness.

• *Cost for rolling over an account.* You may want to find out if you'd have to pay anything for rolling over to another account. If you recall, you can switch your investment options but, if this means heavy fees, you may want to reconsider.

STEP #5: LOOK AT THE FLEXIBILITY OF THE PLAN

You may find that some college plans are more restrictive than others. You want to choose a plan that gives you several investment choices so you can better target your investment according to how far in the future you will need the money. Also, when you think of the flexibility of a plan, also consider how much of a penalty it charges you for moving your money to another state or another plan option.

STEP #6: KEEP GOOD RECORDS

As with all investments, it's important that you keep good records of all your transactions in college savings plans. This is especially important since Congress may revert back to the pre-2001 rules if the tax laws regarding college savings plans are not reaffirmed by 2010.

Coverdell ESA—Saving For Kindergarten To College

The Coverdell Educational Savings Account (Coverdell ESA) was formerly known as the Education Individual Retirement Account (Education IRA) until mid-2001 when the name was changed. The Coverdell ESA is an account that is set up for the purpose of paying educational expenses. Much like college savings plans, the Coverdell ESA is an investment that should be made with your parents' complete involvement.

Think of the Coverdell ESA as a bucket in which you put all kinds of investments—stock, bonds, and other securities. Once the account is established, you can treat it like any other custodial account opened on your behalf for buying and selling stock. What makes a Coverdell ESA so special is that withdrawals from these accounts are not taxed and can be used to pay for elemen-

BOX 17.1
Information on Coverdell ESAs

Internal Revenue Service
www.irs.gov

(Look for Publication 590)

BOX 17.2
The Coverdell ESA At a Glance

Question	Answer
What is a Coverdell ESA?	A savings account that is set up to pay the qualified education expenses of a designated beneficiary.
What types of schools can the Coverdell ESA money be applied to?	Money from a Coverdell ESA is supposed to cover expenses in eligible educational institutions (elementary school, grade school, high school, and college).
Who can a Coverdell ESA be set up for?	Any beneficiary who is under age 18.
Who can contribute to a Coverdell ESA?	Generally, any individual (including the beneficiary) whose Modified Adjust Gross Income (MAGI) for the year is less than $110,000 ($220,000 in the case of a joint return) subject to specified contribution limits.

tary school, grade school, high school, and college expenses such as tuition, computer equipment, and other school-related items. If you are reading this book, however, you are probably in high school so the Coverdell ESA would only be useful for your college expenses. Box 17.2 explains some of the basics of the Coverdell ESA. You and your parents can go to www.teenvestor.com/parents.htm, the section of our website that will give you more complete information about how your parents can help you establish and manage a Coverdell ESA.

Terms that you will frequently hear when people talk about Coverdell ESAs are provided below.

- *Designated beneficiary*. This is the individual named in the document creating the Coverdell ESA who will receive the benefit of the funds in the account. The Coverdell ESA is a custodial account, which means that your parents will have to open the account for you and designate you as the beneficiary. You can still make some of the investment decisions in the account, however, as long as your parents are aware of what you are doing.

• *Qualified educational expenses.* These are expenses required for the enrollment or attendance of the designated beneficiary of the Coverdell ESA at any eligible educational institution. These expenses include tuition, fees, books, supplies, and equipment such as computers, calculators, and other school-related items.

• *Eligible educational institution.* An eligible educational institution is any college, university, vocational school, elementary/secondary (K–12), and other institution eligible to participate in a student aid program administered by the Department of Education. It includes virtually all accredited, public, nonprofit, and private elementary, secondary, and post-secondary institutions. The educational institution should be able to tell you if it is an eligible institution.

• *Contribution limits.* Since 2002, the maximum contribution amount that you can put into the Coverdell ESA account for any one beneficiary can be no more than $2,000. This means that if a beneficiary adds up all the Coverdell ESA accounts opened up for him, the total contribution amount can't be more than $2,000. For example, suppose a girl's grandparents, parents, and godmother each open a Coverdell ESA for her. In order to receive the favorable tax treatment of a Coverdell ESA, the total contribution in all of the accounts opened on her behalf can't be more than $2,000.

DIFFERENCES BETWEEN THE COVERDELL ESA
AND COLLEGE SAVINGS PLANS

Coverdell ESAs are not to be confused with college savings plans. While Coverdell ESAs can certainly be used to pay for college expenses, they are not state-sponsored plans. Perhaps the two most significant features of the Coverdell ESAs that are not features of college savings plans are that:

BOX 17.3

Differences between Coverdell ESA and College Savings Plans

(Your Parents May Be Interested in this Information)

	Coverdell ESA	College Savings Plan
Maximum Contribution in a Year	$2,000	As much as $200,000 in total contributions or higher in some states
Income Limitation of Person Opening Up the Account	Single filer: $110,000 Joint filer: $220,000	None
Use of the Money	For expenses in colleges, universities, vocational school, and grades K–12	For expenses in colleges and universities only.
Who Controls the Investment Decisions	The person who opened the account since the Coverdell ESA is a custodial account	The person who opened the account subject to investment choices offered by the state
Who Owns the Assets in the Account	The person for whom the account was opened	The person who opened the account

• There are income limitations for participants in a Coverdell ESA. Since your parents are the ones that will probably open the account for your benefit, they will have to pay attention to the income limitations described in Box 17.3.

• The funds in a Coverdell ESA can be used for grades K–12 as well as for colleges and universities.

Box 17.3 summarizes the major differences between the Coverdell ESA and college savings plans.

18

Investing in the Coverdell ESA, Step by Step

A Coverdell Educational Savings Account or Coverdell ESA is not an investment but a type of account with which you can buy stocks, mutual funds, and other assets for educational expenses. As we discussed in Chapter 17, the advantage to a Coverdell ESA is that there are tax benefits associated with the investments when withdrawals are made from the account. In order to reap the tax benefits of a Coverdell ESA, the account must be designated as a Coverdell ESA from the start. Once again, the account will probably be established by your parents for your benefit.

STEP #1: DECIDE IF A COVERDELL ESA IS RIGHT FOR YOU VERSUS A COLLEGE SAVINGS PLAN

How Much Control Do You Want? Unlike a college savings plan, you have complete control over the type of investments you can buy for your

Coverdell ESA. By contrast, and as discussed in Chapters 15 and 16, with a college savings plan, you have a limited number of investment choices and you are restricted as to how much you can move your money around from one plan to another.

STEP #2: DETERMINING HOW MUCH YOU ARE ALLOWED TO INVEST IN A COVERDELL ACCOUNT

The maximum anyone can contribute to a Coverdell ESA is $2,000. If your parents are opening the account for your benefit, they have to know how much they can contribute based on their income. They can check the parent's section in our website, www.teenvestor.com/parents.htm, for more guidance on the specific income limitations that can apply to them.

STEP #3: OPEN AN ACCOUNT

If you already have a broker, see if your broker will allow you to open a Coverdell ESA. Most brokers do these days. If your broker does not set up Coverdell ESAs, you are going to have to shop for a new broker. Keep an eye on the fees brokers charge on these accounts. The fees, charges, and expenses will vary based on the investments you select for your Coverdell ESA portfolio and where you open your account. Because the amount you are allowed to contribute is so low (for example, a maximum of $2,000), annual expenses can eat up a big portion of your contributions.

An alternative to opening up a Coverdell ESA with a broker is to open a Coverdell ESA with a large mutual fund company such as Vanguard. As we discussed in Chapter 13, fund companies allow you to open tax-advantaged accounts such as the Coverdell ESA with less money (from $500 to $1,000) than the $2,500 to $3,000 they normally require for regular mutual fund accounts. There are some big mutual fund companies such as Fidelity and Putnam, however, that don't allow you to open Coverdell ESAs.

STEP #4: KEEP GOOD RECORDS

Keeping good records of your transaction will help you keep track of your Coverdell ESA so you know when you have hit your investment limits.

PART
6

Looking into the Future

Individual Retirement Accounts

$$$$	⇒	Recommended Minimum Investment	$500 to $1,000
$$	⇒	Minimum Additional Investment (Optional)	$100 to $300

19

IRAs—Not Just for the Old and Gray

Individual retirement accounts (IRAs) are investment accounts authorized by the government to help you save for your needs later on in life. Most people use their IRAs to plan for retirement but if you are a Teenvestor who thinks retirement is too far off in the future, IRAs are also a way to save for things like a home, some emergency expenses, and even an education. There are 11 types of IRAs, but the most relevant IRAs for Teenvestors is the Roth IRA.

A Teenvestor can open a Roth IRA account (through a custodial account established by his parents, of course) only if he has what's called an *earned income*. Earned income can generally be described as money you earn for providing services to others. For example, if you

BOX 19.1
Information on IRAs

Internal Revenue Service
Publication 590
www.irs.gov

The Motley Fool
www.fool.com

SmartMoney
www.smartmoney.com

169

BOX 19.2
IRAs at a Glance

Question	Answer
What is an IRA?	A retirement savings account with specific tax benefits.
Who can open an IRA?	Anyone who works and receives earned income is allowed to open an IRA.
Where can it be established?	An IRA can be established at a bank or through a brokerage account. You must designate that the account is an IRA account when establishing it.
What kind of investment can be included in an IRA?	Once an IRA account has been opened, you can buy assets such as stocks, bonds, mutual funds, CDs, and other investments for the account.

have a job and you receive a W-2 form at the end of the year for your taxes, this is proof of earned income. But what if you get money for chores around the house or for services you provide to people who live in your neighborhood? Some experts say that these too qualify as earned income as long as you keep good records of the money you received for each service you provided.

The main feature of a Roth IRA is that while the money you put into the account is not tax deductible, the profit you make on the account is not taxable if you meet certain conditions discussed in Chapter 20. IRS Publication 590 is a great guide for all the rules applicable to investing in IRAs, however, some of the specific features of a Roth IRA are as follows:

- *How much can I contribute?* You can currently contribute no more than $3,000 each year to a Roth IRA. Box 19.3 gives you the contribution limits for future taxable years for the Roth IRA. The actual amount you can contribute (as opposed to a general contribution limit of $3,000) will depend on your income. Because the contributions are made with after-tax dollars, there are no imme-

BOX 19.3
Contribution Limits for Roth IRAs

Tax Year	Maximum Annual Contribution
2003	$3,000
2004	$3,000
2005	$4,000
2006	$4,000
2007	$5,000
2008	$5,000
2009	Indexed (i.e. adjusted for inflation)

diate tax benefits. However, in the long run, the earnings in the account are not taxable.

• *Can I withdraw my money early?* Early withdrawal is a feature that should please most Teenvestors. It means that you don't have to wait till you are old and gray to get your hands on some of your money. You can withdraw your contributions (as opposed to the earnings or profit you've made in the account) before you are 59-and-a-half years old without a tax penalty as long as you have had the account opened for five years. You will, however, owe taxes on any earnings or profit (as opposed to contributions) you withdraw before then. Withdrawal of earnings or profit is allowed but only in limited instances including the purchase of a first home.

• *How long can earnings accumulate?* Your earnings can accumulate in the account until you are 59 and a half at which time you can withdraw the money (both your contributions and the earnings or profit in the portfolio) without paying any taxes on it if the account has been open for five years. You don't have to withdraw your money at age 59 and a half, in fact, you can keep contributing to the account until age 70 and a half, and you can keep the money in the account after that age in order to earn more on your investments if you'd like.

20

How to Save with Roth IRAs,
Step by Step

STEP #1: DETERMINE IF YOU ARE ELIGIBLE TO INVEST IN A ROTH IRA

You can invest in a Roth IRA if you can show proof of earned income as we described in the previous chapter. Jobs for which you receive a W-2 form for your taxes are proof that you have earned income. If you don't have a regular job but you get money for providing services to your parents at home or you even have your own business, some financial experts say that you can invest in a Roth IRA if you keep good records of how you have earned that income.

STEP #2: DETERMINE HOW MUCH YOU CAN INVEST IN A ROTH IRA

The maximum amount you can invest in a Roth IRA is the lesser of the two amounts listed below:

1. The investment amounts listed in Box 19.3. For 2003, 2004, and 2005, the amounts you can invest are $3,000, $3,000, and $4,000, respectively.

2. The total amount of income you made during the year.

STEP #3: FIND A FINANCIAL INSTITUTION THAT WILL OPEN A ROTH IRA

The following institutions can help you open a Roth IRA:

• *Banks or credit unions.* Remember, when you invest in a Roth IRA, you are actually opening an account to deposit money to purchase investments. If you want very conservative investments, you probably need look no further than your local bank or credit union for a place to open a Roth IRA, which you can use to purchase Certificates of Deposit and money market investments. You can establish these types of IRAs with as little as $200 or less.

• *Mutual fund companies.* If all you want are the mutual funds of one mutual fund company such as Vanguard in your Roth IRA, you can go directly to that company to establish a Roth IRA with them. In this case, the funds that you deposit in your Roth IRA would be used to purchase mutual fund shares of the company. You can also just as easily establish a Roth IRA with a mutual fund company that has a wide variety of funds. If you are interested in purchasing mutual funds, doing so through an IRA is a good idea because you will find that the minimum balance requirements are often much lower than for investing in regular mutual fund accounts. For example, the investment minimum for a regular Vanguard 500 index mutual fund is $3,000 but for an IRA, it is $1,000. See Box 20.1 for other examples of investment limits for no-load mutual funds.

BOX 20.1
IRA Accounts in No-Load/Low-Balance Index Funds

Fund	Symbol	Index	Minimum Balance for Regular Account	Minimum Balance for IRA	Phone/Website
Vanguard 500 Index	VFINX	S&P 500	$3,000	$1,000	800-871-3879 www.vanguard.com
USAA S&P 500 Index	USSPX	S&P 500	$3,000	$1,000	800-382-8722 www.usaa.com
Scudder S&P 500	SCPIX	S&P 500	$2,500	$500	800-728-3337 www.scudder.com
T. Rowe Price Equity Index 500	PREIX	S&P 500	$2,500	$1,000	800-225-5132 www.troweprice.com
Schwab S&P 500 Fund	SWPIX	S&P 500	$2,500	$1,000	800-435-4000 www.schwab.com
T. Rowe Price Total Market Index	POMIX	Wilshire 5000	$2,500	$1,000	800-225-5132 www.troweprice.com
Vanguard Total Stock Market Index	VTSMX	Wilshire 5000	$3,000	$1,000	800-871-3879 www.vanguard.com
TIAA-CREF Equity Index Fund	TCEIX	Russell 3000	$2,500	$2,000	800-223-1200 www.tiaacref.com
Vanguard Small-Cap Index	NAESX	Russell 2000	$3,000	$1,000	800-871-3879 www.vanguard.com

• *Discount brokers.* If you want to include a combination of stocks and mutual funds in an IRA, you would go to your online discount broker to see if they offer such retirement accounts and offer the varieties of mutual funds and stocks you would want to select for them. Of course, when you choose individual securities to put into your IRA, you pay a commission on each trade. As a start, you can check our list of affordable brokers from Box 9.11.

• *Roth IRA direct investment plans.* If you remember from Chapter 10, direct investment plans allow you to buy shares of stock directly from the company. Look into companies that offer Roth IRA direct investment plans. For example, Exxon Mobil has a Roth IRA direct investment plan.

STEP #4: KEEP GOOD RECORDS

Keep all scraps of paper you get from your IRAs because there may be some tax consequences when you cash in your investments.

The Patriot Bond and Its Cousin

Buying a U.S. Savings Bond is one of the easiest investments a Teenvestor can make. Savings bonds are issued by the U.S. Treasury Department. You can't buy them from or sell them to anyone who is not authorized to sell them by the U.S. Treasury Department. Savings bonds are *registered securities*. This means that they are owned exclusively by the person or persons named on them.

There are two varieties of savings bonds Teenvestors should know about: Series EE (also now known as the Patriot) and Series I. We'll begin by describing the Series EE savings bonds and then continue with how the two bonds differ.

> **BOX 21.1**
> **The Patriot Savings Bond**
>
> The Patriot savings bond is a Series EE savings bond inscribed with the words "Patriot Bond." It was first issued in December 21, 2001, as a way for citizens to support the war efforts against terrorism. Any Series EE savings bond you order will be a Patriot Bond.

SERIES EE SAVINGS BONDS
Interest Rate

• *Zero coupon bond.* The Series EE savings bond is a type of bond called a *zero coupon bond* in which all the interest you earn on it is held for you until you cash it in. Box 21.5 at the end of this chapter shows an example of how the Series EE savings bond earns money yearly.

• *Interest rate.* The Series EE savings bond earns interest based on the five-year U.S. Treasury Department's securities rate, a rate published by the government that can be found in financial papers such as the *Wall Street Journal* or *Investor's Business Daily*. At the time of this writing, the Series EE savings bond had an interest rate of 3.25% compounded every six months.

Affordability

• *Eight denominations.* Series EE savings bonds come in eight denominations (also known as face value)—$50, $75, $100, $200, $500, $1,000, $5,000, and $10,000. With this many options, you can tailor your savings to meet your goals and needs.

• *What you pay.* The amount you'd actually pay for the Series EE savings bond is half the denomination or face value. For example, you can buy a $50 Series EE bond for $25, and the interest you earn will be held for you until it at least doubles your initial investment.

• *Fees.* The U.S. Treasury Department never charges fees when you buy or redeem savings bonds.

Accessibility

- *Six-month wait.* After you buy a savings bond, you are required to wait at least six months before you can get your money back. Once six months have elapsed, you can get your money back plus some interest, although not the full interest you are due.

- *Losing interest.* If you want to cash in your savings bonds before five years have elapsed since you bought the bonds, you will lose three months worth of interest. After five years, you will get the promised interest and you can get your principal back if you'd like.

Maturity Periods

- *Seventeen-year wait.* If you buy a Series EE bond with a face value of $50 for $25, you will have to wait for at least 17 years to get $50 back from the government. The reason you'd get back $50 is that over those 17 years, your interest will pile up with the government so that your $25 grows to $50. See Box 21.5 for an example of how the Series EE savings bond works.

- *You don't have to cash in bonds early.* You don't have to cash in your bonds at the end of 17 years if you don't want to. You can wait an additional 13 years—making it 30 years in total—at which time you can earn additional interest.

Taxes

- *No state and local taxes.* The interest you earn from savings bonds are exempt from all state and local income taxes.

- *Federal taxes due.* You will, however, owe federal income taxes on the interest when you cash them.

BOX 21.3
Restrictions on Cashing in Your Savings Bonds

If You Want to Pull Your Money out in the Following Periods after Buying Treasury Bonds	Can You Get the Full Interest You Were Promised?	Can You Get Your Original Investment Back?
Before six months*	No	No
After six months and before five years	No**	Yes
After five years	Yes	Yes

*You are restricted from taking your money out before the sixth month
**You will lose three months' worth of interest

- *Educational use.* The earnings may be exempt from federal taxes if you use the bonds to pay for college tuition and fees.

Safety

- *Iron-clad safety.* Savings bonds are very safe because they are guaranteed by the U.S. government. Your principal and earned interest are safe and can't be lost because of changes in the stock market or other financial markets.

- *Replaced when lost.* Savings bonds are registered with the U.S. Treasury Department, so if you lose them or they are stolen or destroyed, they can be replaced at no cost to you.

Convenience

- *Buy from financial institutions.* You can buy savings bonds at more than 40,000 financial institutions nationwide. Chances are that your local bank sells them. You can also buy them online with a credit card at Savings Bonds Direct (www.savings

bonds.gov), which is also an excellent website for savings bond information.

• *Automatic deduction from account.* The government offers a program called EasySaver Plan, which allows you to buy savings bonds directly from your checking or savings account.

SERIES I SAVINGS BONDS

Some critics of EE savings bonds complain that the relatively low interest they pay barely keeps ahead of the inflation rate. The Series I savings bond was designed to address this criticism. The Series I savings bond is a type of bond designed for investors seeking to protect themselves against inflation (hence, the "I" in the name of the bond). Like the Series EE savings bond, the Series I savings bond accumulates interest that is paid when the bond is cashed. Besides the adjustment of the rates paid on the Series I savings bonds for the rate of inflation, the major differences between the Series EE savings bonds and the Series I savings bonds are as follows:

• *Issued at face value.* The Series EE savings bonds are sold at half of face value. By contrast, Series I savings bonds are sold at face value. You pay $50 for a $50 bond, and it grows in value with inflation-indexed earnings for up to 30 years.

• *No guaranteed returns.* The Series EE savings bond guarantees that it will reach its face value in 17 years but there is no guaranteed level of earnings with the Series I saving bond.

HOW TO REGISTER SAVINGS BONDS

Registration establishes who is the owner of the bond. Only the person who is registered on the bond can cash the bond. As far as the government

BOX 21.4
Registration Options

Type of Registration	Example of Social Security Number and Names on Bonds	Who Can Cash in the Bond
Single Ownership	123-45-6789 Sue F. Johnston	Only the registered owner can cash in the bond. On the death of the owner, the bond becomes part of the owner's estate.
Co-Ownership	123-45-6789 Sue F. Johnston Or Mark S. Johnston	Either co-owner may cash in the bond without the knowledge or approval of the other. On the death of one co-owner, the other co-owner becomes the sole owner of the bond.
Beneficiary	123-45-6789 Sue F. Johnston POD Mark S. Johnston	Only the owner may cash in the bond during his or her lifetime. A surviving beneficiary automatically becomes the sole owner of the bond. The acronym "POD" means "Paid on Death."

is concerned, if you are not registered, you are not the rightful owner of the bond.

There are several ways to register a savings bond and you can find them all at the government's website, www.savingsbond.gov, and in Box 21.5. For Teenvestors, the only registration method you have to worry about is *single ownership registration.*

Single ownership registration is done when there is only one owner of the bond. For example, single ownership registration occurs when you buy a savings bond for yourself and put your own Social Security number on the registration form or when, say, a grandparent registers the savings bonds for you by putting your name and Social Security number on the bond. For all ownership types, the person who is registering it has to give an address where the savings bond will be mailed.

Registration is helpful in replacing lost, stolen, or destroyed savings

BOX 21.5*
How Series EE Savings Bonds Work

Series EE savings bonds are sold for half their face value and, when they mature, you get the full face value.

For example, suppose you buy a Series EE savings bond with a face value of $200. Your purchase price for the bond would be $100, half the face value. If you are promised a rate of 3.25%*, here is how your money will stack up over the next 25 years.

Year	Beginning Investment ($)	Interest($)	End Investment ($)
1	100.00	3.25	103.25
2	103.25	3.36	106.61
3	106.61	3.46	110.07
4	110.07	3.58	113.65
5	113.65	3.69	117.34
6	117.34	3.81	121.15
7	121.15	3.94	125.09
8	125.09	4.07	129.16
9	129.16	4.20	133.36
10	133.36	4.33	137.69
11	137.69	4.47	142.16
12	142.16	4.62	146.78
13	146.78	4.77	151.56
14	151.56	4.93	156.48
15	156.48	5.09	161.57
16	161.57	5.25	166.82
17	166.82	5.42	172.24
18	172.24	5.60	177.84
19	177.84	5.78	183.62
20	183.62	5.97	189.58
21	189.58	6.16	195.75
22	195.75	6.36	202.11
23	202.11	6.57	208.68
24	208.68	6.78	215.46
25	215.46	7.00	222.46

*3.25% is compounded annually here but, in reality, it is compounded twice a year

The interest you earn on your investment stays in the account. The government promises you that you will get twice your money back within 17 years. If your money has not doubled in that period, they will top it off so you get twice your original investment.

In our example, the ending balance in the seventeenth year is $172.24—

(continued)

$27.76 short of the $200 promised by the government. If you want your money at the end of the seventeenth year, the government will give you the $200 you were promised.

You don't have to cash in your bonds in the seventeenth year. You can continue to earn interest until the thirtieth year if you'd like. After the thirtieth year, you will stop earning interest so you should withdraw your money.

Pop Quiz—Without doing the same calculations we did above, how long will it take to double your $100 investment if the interest rate is 3.25%?

Answer—Using the Rule of 72 (as described in Chapter 2), the calculation is as follows:

$$\text{Time to Double Money} = 72 \div 3.25 = 22.2 \text{ years}$$

Our table showed that the money is doubled around the twenty-second year (with an ending balance of $202.11).

bonds, and in finding the owners of savings bonds that have stopped earning interest (for example, 30 years have elapsed).

THE USEFULLNESS OF SAVINGS BONDS

Whether to invest in U.S. Savings Bonds or not depends on each Teenvestor's individual circumstances. We recommend that no Teenvestor put all her money in stocks or bonds (or bond-like products like Certificates of Deposit). A mixture of stocks and bonds, however, can give Teenvestors the potential to reap the higher returns of stocks while at the same time offsetting the riskiness of a downturn in the market with the safety afforded by bonds like U.S. savings bonds. For us, it's just not the conservative investor, but a prudent investor, who diversifies his portfolio to include bonds. For the Teenvestor, a good diversification strategy should include Series EE or Series I savings bonds in their portfolio. When you have enough money, you can consider U.S. Treasury Bonds but that's beyond the scope of this book. In the next chapter, we will look at the steps that you will need to take to invest in U.S. savings bonds.

22

Buying U.S. Savings Bonds, Step by Step

The government has made it incredibly easy to buy U.S. Savings Bonds. You can buy them at thousands of banks across the country or even through payroll deductions if your parents' companies participate in the EasySaver program.

STEP #1: GO TO WWW.SAVINGSBONDS.GOV

The U.S. government website, www.savingsbond.gov, is the best website for savings bond information and purchases. Unless you have access to a credit card, you should request online that an order form be mailed to you so you can order a savings bond via the mail. Once you enter the website, you will see a menu of options on the main body of the page with the following headings: "Product Information," "Online Services," "Why Buy

> **BOX 22.1**
> **Savings Bonds as Gifts**
>
> When buying savings bonds as gifts, be sure to have the correct Social Security number and spelling of the recipient's name. If you don't know the recipient's Social Security number, use your own number. The Social Security number is used only for record-keeping purposes. When the bond is cashed in by the recipient, the paying agent will get the recipient's Social Security number at that time to use for tax-reporting purposes.
>
> You can use the "Mail to" section on the bond purchase order if you wish to receive the gift bond so that you can present it to the recipient yourself. When buying a bond as a gift, ask for a free gift certificate.

Bonds?" "How to Buy Bonds," "What Are Your Bonds Worth?," "Fun Calculators," "FAQs," "Contacts," and "Just for Kids."

Step #2: Identify the Current Interest Rates

On the first page of the website, you will see the interest rate for the Series EE (also known as the Patriot) and the Series I savings bonds. You should at least know what you will earn when you put your money in savings bonds. At the time of this writing, the interest rate for the Series EE and Series I savings bonds were 3.25% and 4.08%, respectively. These rates may sound low to you but remember that investing in U.S. Savings Bonds is only one way of diversifying your investment portfolio. Stocks are great but obviously riskier than bonds. For this reason, you may not want 100% of your money invested in stocks.

STEP #3: DECIDE WHICH SAVINGS BOND YOU WANT

Beginning investors who have very little money to invest may want to start with the Series EE savings bond since that requires an investment of half the face value amount. For example, if you want to buy a Series EE savings bond with a face value of $200, you only need to invest $100. A Series I savings bond with a face value of $200 will cost you $200.

STEP #4: ORDER ONLINE (IF YOU CAN)

To order online, you will need access to one of the following: American Express, Visa, MasterCard, or Discover. Ask your parents if they can order it for you online if you don't want to deal with filling out an application and mailing it in. On the main page, under the section "How to Buy Bonds," choose the option, "Savings Bonds Direct (Buy Online)." Once again, even if the site is changed, you should still easily find the section for online ordering of savings bonds. The application process is very simple. To complete the application process, you will need to know:

1. **Type of bond.** The type of bond you want to buy and its denomination. You can buy Series EE and Series I savings bonds in (face value) denominations of $50, $100, $200, and so on.

2. **Owner information.** The owner is the intended recipient of the bond, the person who you want to eventually cash in the savings bond. Whether your parents are ordering it for you or you are ordering it for yourself, you should put your name and your Social Security number in the owner information section.

3. **Ownership option.** The most common ownership option is the single owner option. You would select this option if you are buying the bond for yourself. If your parents are buying it on your behalf, they should also select the single owner option. The co-owner option should be selected if you want two people to own the bond jointly (for example, for yourself and a parent or sibling). Either co-owner can cash in the bond without getting permission from

the other co-owner. The beneficiary option is if you want someone else to get the bond in case you die.

4. **Delivery address.** You will be asked to enter the name and address of the person to whom the savings bond is to be delivered.

STEP #5: ORDER AN APPLICATION IF YOU ARE NOT ABLE TO ORDER THE BONDS ONLINE

As we noted earlier, you can have an application mailed to you if you are not able to order online. In the "Product Information" section of the homepage of the site, select the "Forms" option. Even if the website has been slightly changed, you should still be able to find the section where you can order the forms you need.

STEP #6: KEEP GOOD RECORDS

We recommend that each time you make a purchase of a savings bond, you record the issue date, serial number (with prefix and suffix), face value, and amount you paid. A table is provided in Box 22.2 to help you keep track of your savings bond transactions.

BOX 22.2
Savings Bond Transactions

Issue Date (Month/Year)	Serial Number (with Prefix and Suffix)	Face Value	Amount Invested	Date Cashed	Amount Received when Cashed In

Show Me the Money!: Two Prominent Company Scandals Explained

ENRON

On December 2, 2001, Enron—a Fortune 500 company with over $130 billion in sales—filed for Chapter 11 bankruptcy. This is the second biggest bankruptcy ever in the United States.

Chapter 11 bankruptcy gives Enron breathing room so it can negotiate with those it owes money (for example, its creditors). It stops these creditors from taking any drastic actions to collect money from Enron. Under a Chapter 11 bankruptcy, Enron can maintain control of its assets.

For all practical purposes, Enron, as we once knew it, has collapsed. This is a company that had a market capitalization of about $60 billion in early 2001 and whose stock was as high as $84.88 (within a year before its bankruptcy). As of year-end 2002, Enron's stock was worth less than a penny. Investors can still buy the company's stock but, if they do, they are taking a big risk since no one knows for sure if the company will survive.

You may be wondering how a company that was the seventh largest on the Fortune 500 list in 2000 could fall so quickly and so far. The government is looking at the possibility of sleazy financial dealings.

The collapse of Enron provides a valuable lesson to Teenvestors and other beginning investors. The lesson is that one should understand the type of business in which he or she is investing. It sounds like a silly statement but this is the philosophy of investment experts such as Peter Lynch and Warren Buffett.

You are probably saying to yourself that surely Wall Street experts knew what Enron officials were up to. You'd be surprised that many of these so-called experts weren't really sure how Enron was making its money. As long as Enron showed steady profits every year, they looked the other way.

Ken Lay formed Enron in 1985 after merging two gas pipeline companies. Initially, the company made its money by delivering energy to its customers via pipelines. By 2000, 80% of the company's sales were from what Enron called "wholesale energy operations." What this translated to was that the company had become more of a financial trading company (trading in energy-related products) much like investment banks such as Merrill Lynch and Goldman Sachs. So you see, an investment in Enron was less and less an investment in an energy/utility company, and more of an investment in a company that traded sophisticated financial instruments. But the problem was that Enron was not a strong enough company to be in that type of trading business.

Enron also found innovative ways of hiding how much debt it really had on its balance sheet. Let's discuss this issue of hiding debt for a minute. If you know anything about trying to decide how strong a company is, you must know that you have to find out how much money the company has borrowed. (Our book, *Teenvestor®: The Practical Investment Guide for Teens and Their Parents* covers this in great detail). To quickly summarize the importance of debt, consider what happens when your parents want to borrow money from a bank for a car, for a house, for school, or for other purposes. One of the first things the bank will want to know is whether your parents have borrowed money from other people. The logic is that if your parents owe other people too much money, they may not be able to pay those people back and also pay back the money they owe on the new loan they are requesting from the bank.

But what if your parents were able to somehow arrange their finances such that the bank is not able to tell whether they have borrowed money from other people. For example, suppose one of your relatives lent your parents money without anyone else knowing about it and without any financial records showing how much money they borrowed. Your parents still have to pay the relative back; it's just that there are no financial records to show that the loan was made to your parents.

You can see that in this situation, the bank may lend your parents money because they are not aware of their other debt (for example, the money your parents owe your relative). If after the bank makes the loan it finds out that your parents had previously borrowed money from the relative, the bank would be worried that your parents may not be able to pay everyone back. If the bank never finds out about your parents' other loans and if your parents keep making payments on all their loans, everyone is happy. But what happens if one of your parents loses his or her job. Your family now has to decide which debt to pay first (if you have any money at all to pay anyone back). This is exactly the situation that banks and other creditors try to avoid. They want to make sure that even if your financial condition changes, you can still make the payments on loans.

The example we discussed above is one form of *off-balance-sheet financing*. The borrowing is off-balance-sheet because it would not show up on your parents' personal balance sheets. (Balance sheets show what an individual owes and what he owns.) Enron also used its own methods of off-balance-sheet financing to blur how much money it really owed. Here is a quote from the *New York Times* (Sunday, December 23, 2001) about this type of financing:

> *In itself, off-balance-sheet financing is no vice. Companies can use it in perfectly legitimate ways that carry little risk to shareholders. The trouble is, while more companies are relying on off-balance-sheet methods to finance their operations, investors are usually unaware that a company with a clean balance sheet may be loaded with debt—until it is too late.*

Through its trading operations (which made use of complex financial transactions), Enron engaged in off-balance-sheet financing. However, the company kept denying at every step that it was looking more and more like a trading company. In a February 2001, interview with *Fortune* writer Bethany McLean, here is what then-CFO Andy Fastow said:

> *We are not a trading company. We are not in the business of making money by speculating.*

We now know this was not entirely true. In that same interview session, then-CEO Jeff Skilling of Enron had an interesting quote that speaks volumes about the difficulty many people had in understanding the company's business:

> *Our business is not a black box. It's very simple to model. People who raise questions are people who have not gone through it in detail. We have explicit answers but people want to throw rocks at us.*

Truth is, investors didn't really understand what Enron was doing. In addition, many so-called experts either didn't want to look dumb by continuing to ask for the simplest of explanations or they turned a blind eye to questionable practices in order to make a profit by doing business with Enron.

WORLDCOM

With about $104 billion in assets, WorldCom is the largest bankruptcy ever filed in United States. WorldCom's problem hit a crescendo when it was discovered that the company deceived the public about its earnings. Instead of making $1.4 billion in 2001 and $172 million in the first quarter of 2002, the company admitted that it actually lost money the whole time. In total, the company booked about $9 billion more in revenue over several years than it should have.

Exactly how did WorldCom deceive the public and all those Wall Street analysts? First, let's go over some very basic accounting principles.

Let's suppose you own a furniture store. When you buy office supplies like paper, pencils, and other inexpensive items for your business, you are required to subtract these expenses from the money you take in from customers (your revenue) in order to calculate the profit you make each year. The basic formula is as follows:

Profit = Revenue - Expenses

But what if you buy a big expensive truck costing, say, $200,000, which you will use to haul furniture to your customers? Since you will probably use the truck over a number of years in your business, it doesn't make sense to consider the truck as if the expense were in the same category as the office supply expense. The office supplies like pens and pencils last a short time; they will probably be used up in a year. The truck, on the other hand, will last years, so it makes sense to allocate the cost of the truck over the number of years you'll use it.

For example, if you think the truck will last 20 years, it means that you will use up $10,000 of the truck every year, calculated as follows:

Cost per Year = Total Cost of Big Expense ÷ # of Years of Use You'll Get Out of It
Cost per Year = $200,000 ÷ 20 years = $10,000 per year

The tax laws would let you count only $10,000 of expenses associated with the truck each year.

Now back to WorldCom! What the company did was similar to having expenses like the office supplies we mentioned earlier but treating them as you would treat a big expense like the truck. In other words, instead of subtracting some expenses from their revenue in the year in which they spent the money, they only subtracted a part of it, in essence claiming that those expenses should be spread across several years. This artificially reduces the company's true expenses and, thereby, artificially boosted its profits.

To put it simply, WorldCom made their pencil expenses look like a truck expense and, in the process, made their profit look better than it actually was.

Appendix II

General Requirements for the Direct Investment Plans of the Companies in the Dow

(Read Plan Details for Up-to-Date Requirements)

We've listed basic requirements for the Dow companies that offer direct investment plans. Many of the companies charge a one-time setup fee that ranges from $5 to $20. In addition, if you agree to have money taken out of your account periodically, in some cases, the fees for making optional cash investments can be cut in half.

Direct investment plans change frequently so it's important that you read the prospectus for the plan in which you'd like to invest. At the very least, you should go to the websites that we listed in Box 11.2 for quick information about current plan provisions. Also, our website, www.teenvestor.com/drips.htm, can also help you keep up to date.

ALCOA (AA)

Must you own shares registered in your name before enrolling?   **Yes**
How many shares must be registered in your name before enrolling?   I
What is the minimum deposit to the company if you don't have to own registered shares before enrolling?   **Not Applicable**
What is the minimum optional cash investment once you enroll?   **$25**
Fee for making optional cash investment: **$0**
Fee for selling shares: **$10**

Website: **www.alcoa.com**
Number for plan materials: 800-317-4445

AMERICAN EXPRESS (AXP)

Must you own shares registered in your name before enrolling?   **No**
How many shares must be registered in your name before enrolling?   **Not Applicable**
What is the minimum deposit to the company if you don't have to own registered shares before enrolling? **$1,000**
What is the minimum optional cash investment once you enroll? **$50**
Fee for making optional cash investment: **$5**
Fee for selling shares: **$10**
Website: **www.americanexpress.com**
Number for plan materials: 800-842-7629

AT&T (T)

Must you own shares registered in your name before enrolling?   **Yes**
How many shares must be registered in your name before enrolling?   1
What is the minimum deposit to the company if you don't have to own registered shares before enrolling?   **Not Applicable**
What is the minimum optional cash investment once you enroll? **$100**
Fee for making optional cash investment: **$5**
Fee for selling shares: **$20**
Website: **www.att.com**
Number for plan materials: 800-348-8288

BOEING (BA)

Must you own shares registered in your name before enrolling?   **Yes**
How many shares must be registered in your name before enrolling?   50
What is the minimum deposit to the company if you don't have to own registered shares before enrolling?   **Not Applicable**
What is the minimum optional cash investment once you enroll? **$50**
Fee for making optional cash investment: **$1**
Fee for selling shares: **$10**
Website: **www.boeing.com**
Number for plan materials: 888-777-0923

CATERPILLAR (CAT)

Must you own shares registered in your name before enrolling?   **No**
How many shares must be registered in your name before enrolling?   **Not Applicable**
What is the minimum deposit to the company if you don't have to own registered shares before enrolling?   **$500**

What is the minimum optional cash investment once you enroll? $50
Fee for making optional cash investment: $5
Fee for selling shares: $15
Website: www.cat.com
Number for plan materials: 800-446-2617

COCA-COLA (KO)
Must you own shares registered in your name before enrolling?   **Yes**
How many shares must be registered in your name before enrolling?   1
What is the minimum deposit to the company if you don't have to own registered
 shares before enrolling?   **Not Applicable**
What is the minimum optional cash investment once you enroll? $10
Fee for making optional cash investment: $0
Fee for selling shares: $15
Website: www.cocacola.com
Number for plan materials: 888-265-3747

DUPONT (DD)
Must you own shares registered in your name before enrolling?   **Yes**
How many shares must be registered in your name before enrolling?   1
What is the minimum deposit to the company if you don't have to own registered
 shares before enrolling?   **Not Applicable**
What is the minimum optional cash investment once you enroll? $20
Fee for making optional cash investment: $3
Fee for selling shares: $10
Website: www.dupont.com
Number for plan materials: 888-983-8766

EASTMAN KODAK (EK)
Must you own shares registered in your name before enrolling?   **No**
How many shares must be registered in your name before enrolling?   **Not Applicable**
What is the minimum deposit to the company if you don't have to own registered
 shares before enrolling? $150
What is the minimum optional cash investment once you enroll? $50
Fee for making optional cash investment: $5
Fee for selling shares: $15
Website: www.kodak.com
Number for plan materials: 800-253-6057

EXXON MOBIL (XOM)

Must you own shares registered in your name before enrolling?   **No**

How many shares must be registered in your name before enrolling?   **Not Applicable**

What is the minimum deposit to the company if you don't have to own registered shares before enrolling?   **$250**

What is the minimum optional cash investment once you enroll?   **$50**

Fee for making optional cash investment: **$0**

Fee for selling shares: **$5**

Website: **www.exxonmobil.com**

Number for plan materials: **800-252-1800**

GENERAL ELECTRIC (GE)

Must you own shares registered in your name before enrolling?   **No**

How many shares must be registered in your name before enrolling?   **Not Applicable**

What is the minimum deposit to the company if you don't have to own registered shares before enrolling?   **$250**

What is the minimum optional cash investment once you enroll?   **$10**

Fee for making optional cash investment: **$3**

Fee for selling shares: **$10**

Website: **www.ge.com**

Number for plan materials: **800-786-2543**

GENERAL MOTORS (GM)

Must you own shares registered in your name before enrolling?   **Yes**

How many shares must be registered in your name before enrolling?   **1**

What is the minimum deposit to the company if you don't have to own registered shares before enrolling?   **Not Applicable**

What is the minimum optional cash investment once you enroll?   **$25**

Fee for making optional cash investment: **$0**

Fee for selling shares: **$15**

Website: **www.gm.com**

Number for plan materials: **800-331-9922**

HOME DEPOT (HD)

Must you own shares registered in your name before enrolling?   **No**

How many shares must be registered in your name before enrolling?   **Not Applicable**

What is the minimum deposit to the company if you don't have to own registered shares before enrolling?   **$250**

What is the minimum optional cash investment once you enroll?   **$25**

Fee for making optional cash investment: **$2.50**

Fee for selling shares: **$10**

Website: **www.homedepot.com**
Number for plan materials: 800-577-0177

HONEYWELL (HON)
Must you own shares registered in your name before enrolling? **Yes**
How many shares must be registered in your name before enrolling? 1
What is the minimum deposit to the company if you don't have to own registered shares before enrolling? **Not Applicable**
What is the minimum optional cash investment once you enroll? $25
Fee for making optional cash investment: $0
Fee for selling shares: **Not Available**
Website: **www.honeywell.com**
Number for plan materials: 800-647-7147

INTEL (INTC)
Must you own shares registered in your name before enrolling? **Yes**
How many shares must be registered in your name before enrolling? 1
What is the minimum deposit to the company if you don't have to own registered shares before enrolling? **Not Applicable**
What is the minimum optional cash investment once you enroll? $50
Fee for making optional cash investment: $4
Fee For selling shares: $4
Website: **www.intc.com**
Number for plan materials: 800-298-0146

INTERNATIONAL BUSINESS MACHINES (IBM)
Must you own shares registered in your name before enrolling? No
How many shares must be registered in your name before enrolling? **Not Applicable**
What is the minimum deposit to the company if you don't have to own registered shares before enrolling? $500
What is the minimum optional cash investment once you enroll? $50
Fee for making optional cash investment: $5
Fee for selling shares: $15
Website: **www.ibm.com**
Number for plan materials: 888-426-6700

INTERNATIONAL PAPER
Must you own shares registered in your name before enrolling? No
How many shares must be registered in your name before enrolling? **Not Applicable**
What is the minimum deposit to the company if you don't have to own registered shares before enrolling? $500

What is the minimum optional cash investment once you enroll? $50
Fee for making optional cash investment: $0
Fee for selling shares: $15
Website: www.ipaper.com
Number for plan materials: 800-678-8715

J.P. MORGAN CHASE (JPM)
Must you own shares registered in your name before enrolling?   **Yes**
How many shares must be registered in your name before enrolling?   1
What is the minimum deposit to the company if you don't have to own registered shares before enrolling?   **Not Applicable**
What is the minimum optional cash investment once you enroll? $0
Fee for making optional cash investment: $0
Fee for selling shares: **Not Available**
Website: **www.chase.com**
Number for plan materials: 800-758-4651

JOHNSON & JOHNSON (JNJ)
Must you own shares registered in your name before enrolling?   **Yes**
How many shares must be registered in your name before enrolling?   1
What is the minimum deposit to the company if you don't have to own registered shares before enrolling?   **Not Applicable**
What is the minimum optional cash investment once you enroll? $25
Fee for making optional cash investment: $0
Fee for selling shares: $15
Website: **www.jnj.com**
Number for plan materials: 800-328-9033

MCDONALD'S (MCD)
Must you own shares registered in your name before enrolling?   No
How many shares must be registered in your name before enrolling?   **Not Applicable**
What is the minimum deposit to the company if you don't have to own registered shares before enrolling? $500
What is the minimum optional cash investment once you enroll? $50
Fee for making optional cash investment: $6
Fee for selling shares: $15
Website: **www.mcdonalds.com**
Number for plan materials: 800-621-7825

MERCK (MRK)

Must you own shares registered in your name before enrolling?   No
How many shares must be registered in your name before enrolling?   **Not Applicable**
What is the minimum deposit to the company if you don't have to own registered
    shares before enrolling? $350
What is the minimum optional cash investment once you enroll? $50
Fee for making optional cash investment: $5
Fee for selling shares: $5
Website: **www.merck.com**
Number for plan materials: 800-831-8248

3M (MMM)

Must you own shares registered in your name before enrolling?   **Yes**
How many shares must be registered in your name before enrolling?   1
What is the minimum deposit to the company if you don't have to own registered
    shares before enrolling?   **Not Applicable**
What is the minimum optional cash investment once you enroll? $10
Fee for making optional cash investment: $0
Fee for selling shares: **Not Available**
Website: **www.3m.com**
Number for plan materials: 800-401-1952

PHILIP MORRIS (MO)

Must you own shares registered in your name before enrolling?   **Yes**
How many shares must be registered in your name before enrolling?   1
What is the minimum deposit to the company if you don't have to own registered
    shares before enrolling?   **Not Applicable**
What is the minimum optional cash investment once you enroll? $10
Fee for making optional cash investment: $0
Fee for selling shares: $10
Website: **www.philipmorris.com**
Number for plan materials: 800-442-0077

PROCTER & GAMBLE (PG)

Must you own shares registered in your name before enrolling?   No
How many shares must be registered in your name before enrolling?   **Not Applicable**
What is the minimum deposit to the company if you don't have to own registered
    shares before enrolling? $250
What is the minimum optional cash investment once you enroll? $100
Fee for making optional cash investment: $2.50
Fee for selling shares: $2.50

Website: **www.pg.com**
Number for plan materials: 800-764-7483

SBC COMMUNICATIONS (SBC)
Must you own shares registered in your name before enrolling? **No**
How many shares must be registered in your name before enrolling? **Not Applicable**
What is the minimum deposit to the company if you don't have to own registered shares before enrolling? **$500**
What is the minimum optional cash investment once you enroll? **$50**
Fee for making optional cash investment: **$2.50**
Fee for selling shares: **$10**
Website: **www.sbc.com**
Number for plan materials: 800-351-7221

UNITED TECHNOLOGIES (UTX)
Must you own shares registered in your name before enrolling? **Yes**
How many shares must be registered in your name before enrolling? **10**
What is the minimum deposit to the company if you don't have to own registered shares before enrolling? **Not Applicable**
What is the minimum optional cash investment once you enroll? **$100**
Fee for making optional cash investment: **$0**
Fee for selling shares: **$10**
Website: **www.utc.com**
Number for plan materials: 800-519-3111

WALT DISNEY (DIS)
Must you own shares registered in your name before enrolling? **No**
How many shares must be registered in your name before enrolling? **Not Applicable**
What is the minimum deposit to the company if you don't have to own registered shares before enrolling? **$1,000**
What is the minimum optional cash investment once you enroll? **$100**
Fee for making optional cash investment: **$5**
Fee for selling shares: **$10**
Website: **www.disney.com**
Number for plan materials: 818-553-7200

WAL-MART (WMT)
Must you own shares registered in your name before enrolling? **No**
How many shares must be registered in your name before enrolling? **Not Applicable**
What is the minimum deposit to the company if you don't have to own registered shares before enrolling? **$250**

What is the minimum optional cash investment once you enroll? $50
Fee for making optional cash investment: $5
Fee for selling shares: $20
Website: **www.wal-mart.com**
Number for plan materials: **800-438-6278**

Appendix III

**Excerpts from the prospectus of
The Vanguard 500 Index Fund**

Vanguard® Small-Cap Index Fund
SUPPLEMENT TO THE PROSPECTUS DATED APRIL 26, 2002

Effective July 1, 2002, the Small-Cap Index Fund has switched from a sampling method of indexing to the replication method. Accordingly, rather than investing in a representative sample of securities included in the Russell 2000 Index, the Fund will now hold each security found in the Index in about the same proportion as represented in the Index itself.

Fund Profile—
Vanguard® Total Stock Market Index Fund

INVESTMENT OBJECTIVE

The Fund seeks to match the performance of a benchmark index that measures the investment return of the overall stock market.

PRIMARY INVESTMENT STRATEGIES

The Fund employs a passive management strategy designed to track the performance of the Wilshire 5000 Total Market Index, which consists of all the U.S. common stocks regularly traded on the New York and American Stock Exchanges and the Nasdaq over-the-counter market. The Fund invests all or substantially all of its assets in a representative sample of the stocks that make up the Index. For a description of the Fund's sampling technique, please see "Indexing Methods" under **More on the Funds**.

PRIMARY RISK

An investment in the Fund could lose money over short or even long periods. You should expect the Fund's share price and total return to fluctuate within a wide range, like the fluctuations of the overall stock market.

PERFORMANCE/RISK INFORMATION

The following bar chart and table are intended to help you understand the risks of investing in the Fund. The bar chart shows how the performance of the Fund's Investor Shares has varied from one calendar year to another over the periods shown. The table shows how the average annual total returns compare with those of the Fund's target index. Keep in mind that the Fund's past performance does not indicate how it will perform in the future.

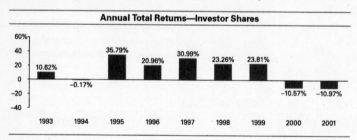

Annual Total Returns—Investor Shares

During the periods shown in the bar chart, the highest return for a calendar quarter was 21.51% (quarter ended December 31, 1998), and the lowest return for a quarter was −15.93% (quarter ended September 30, 2001).

Average Annual Total Returns for Periods Ended December 31, 2001			
	1 Year	5 Years	Since Inception*
Vanguard Total Stock Market Index Fund Investor Shares	−10.97%	9.74%	12.73%
Wilshire 5000 Index	−10.96	9.69	12.89
*April 27, 1992.			

FEES AND EXPENSES

The following table describes the fees and expenses you may pay if you buy and hold Investor Shares of the Fund. The expenses shown under *Annual Fund Operating Expenses* are based on those incurred in the fiscal year ended December 31, 2001.

SHAREHOLDER FEES *(fees paid directly from your investment)*

Sales Charge (Load) Imposed on Purchases:	None
Purchase Fee:	None*
Sales Charge (Load) Imposed on Reinvested Dividends:	None
Redemption Fee:	None
Exchange Fee:	None

ANNUAL FUND OPERATING EXPENSES *(expenses deducted from the Fund's assets)*

Management Expenses:	0.18%
12b-1 Distribution Fee:	None
Other Expenses:	0.02%
Total Annual Fund Operating Expenses:	**0.20%**

*The Fund reserves the right to deduct a purchase fee from future purchases of shares.

The following example is intended to help you compare the cost of investing in the Fund's Investor Shares with the cost of investing in other mutual funds. It illustrates the hypothetical expenses that you would incur over various periods if you invest $10,000 in the Fund's shares. This example assumes that the Fund provides a return of 5% a year and that operating expenses remain the same. The results apply whether or not you redeem your investment at the end of the given period.

1 Year	3 Years	5 Years	10 Years
$20	$64	$113	$255

This example should not be considered to represent actual expenses or performance from the past or for the future. Actual future expenses may be higher or lower than those shown.

Additional Information

Dividends and Capital Gains
Dividends are distributed quarterly in March, June, September, and December; capital gains, if any, are distributed annually in December.

Investment Adviser
The Vanguard Group, Valley Forge, Pa., since inception

Inception Date
April 27, 1992

Net Assets (all share classes) as of December 31, 2001
$25 billion

Newspaper Abbreviation
TotSt

Vanguard Fund Number
85

Cusip Number
922908306

Ticker Symbol
VTSMX

	Vanguard Small-Cap Growth Index Fund Investor Shares Year Ended December 31,			
	2001	**2000**	**1999**	**1998***
Net Asset Value, Beginning of Period	**$10.97**	**$11.38**	**$ 9.53**	**$10.00**
Investment Operations				
Net Investment Income	.009	.009	.025	.03
Net Realized and Unrealized Gain (Loss) on Investments	(.094)	.154	1.860	(.47)
Total from Investment Operations	(.085)	.163	1.885	(.44)
Distributions				
Dividends from Net Investment Income	(.015)	(.003)	(.035)	(.03)
Distributions from Realized Capital Gains	—	(.570)	—	—
Total Distributions	(.015)	(.573)	(.035)	(.03)
Net Asset Value, End of Period	**$10.87**	**$10.97**	**$11.38**	**$ 9.53**
Total Return**	**–0.78%**	**1.59%**	**19.80%**	**–4.77%**
Ratios/Supplemental Data				
Net Assets, End of Period (Millions)	$357	$356	$167	$90
Ratio of Total Expenses to Average Net Assets	0.27%	0.27%	0.25%	0.25%†
Ratio of Net Investment Income to Average Net Assets	0.11%	0.03%	0.33%	0.63%†
Turnover Rate	74%	136%	82%	77%

*Subscription period for the Fund was April 20, 1998, to May 20, 1998, during which time all assets were held in money market instruments. Performance measurement began May 21, 1998.
**Total return figures do not reflect the purchase fee (0.5% from March 1, 1999, through March 31, 2002; 1.0% from inception through February 28, 1999).
†Annualized.

For Your Parents: Table for Comparing
Tax-Advantaged Investment Options

(IRAs, College Plans, ESAs, Custodial Accounts)
see www.teenvestor.com/various_accounts.com for updates

Maximum Investment	Roth IRA	Coverdell ESA	College Savings Plans (529 Plans)	Custodial Accounts
	Up to $3,000 per person per year (up to $5,000 in 2008) for all IRAs combined. Your adjusted gross income (AGI) will determine how much you can contribute.	$2,000 per child.	It varies from state to state depending on projected increases in the state's tuition. Up to $200,000 in some states—in Pennsylvania, up to $260,000.	Unlimited, but "kiddie tax" applies if account earns more than $1,400. Gift tax may also apply.
Who Has Legal Ownership?	The individual who established the account.	The beneficiary is the legal owner of the account, but control stays in the hands of the person who established the account (the custodian).	The person who established the account is the account owner. The person who will be going to college is the beneficiary, but control stays in the hands of the account owner.	The child owns the account, but control is in the hands of the custodian. When the child reaches majority age (18 or more), he takes control of the account.

Maximum Investment	Roth IRA	Coverdell ESA	College Savings Plans (529 Plans)	Custodial Accounts
Investment Flexibility	Very high.	High. Can choose between mutual funds, stocks, bonds and other investments.	Low. You are often limited to a handful of investment choices.	Very high. You can put money in any number of investments. Money can even be moved to 529 plans in most states and transferred to another beneficiary.
Income Limits	Adjusted gross income for singles is less than or equal to $110,000. Adjusted gross income for those who are married is less than or equal to $160,000.	Joint income is less than $220,000.	None	None
Reasons You or Your Estate Can Legally Take a Distribution (Both Contribution and Earnings) from the Investment.	Contributions can be taken out any time without penalty. To withdraw earnings as well, you must have had the account for 5 years and: 1) You have expenses associated with first home purchase; 2) You are 59.5; 3) You become disabled; or 4) Payment is made to your beneficary (or your estate) after your death.	Qualified elementary, high school or higher-education expenses.	Qualified higher Education Expensees (i.e college expenses).	For any reason that benefits the child.
Penalties for Early/Unqualified Withdrawals or for Not Using Money for Intended Purpose	Taxes on earnings and 10% penalty on earnings.	Taxes on earnings and 10% penalty on earnings.	Taxes on earnings and 10% penalty on earnings. There may be additional state penalties.	IRS could tax earnings at parents' rate and there may be additional penalties.
Are Contributions Tax Deductible?	No.	No.	No.	No.
Are Earings Tax Free?	Yes.	Yes.	Yes.	If account is for kids under 14, 1st $750 is tax free. Otherwise, no.
Can You Take Early Distributions Without Penalty?	Yes.	No.	No.	Not applicable—just like a regular investment account.
Age You Can take Penalty-Free Withdrawals on Contributions or Earnings	Anytime for contributions. You must wait till 59.5 withdraw earnings.	Anytime as long as child is in qualified educational institution.	Anytime as long as child is enrolled in higher education.	Anytime for qualified withdrawals—i.e. if it is for the child's benefit.

Maximum Investment	Roth IRA	Coverdell ESA	College Savings Plans (529 Plans)	Custodial Accounts
Age You Must Take Penalty-Free Withdrawals on Earnings	You don't have to take withdrawals.	During a child's enrollment in qualified educational institution.	During a child's enrollment in qualified educational institution. Alternatively, you can transfer money to account of a "relative" as defined by IRS.	Not applicable—money belongs to minor when he/she reaches majority age.
Max. Age You Can Keep Contributing	Can contribute beyond age 70.5 as long as you have earned income.	Not applicable—you can contribute as long as beneficiary is 18 years or younger.	Not applicable—you can contribute as long as beneficiary is 18 years or younger. Of course, you can transfer account to a "relative" and keep contributing. however, maximum contribution limits still apply.	Not applicable—you typically open up a custodial account for minors.
Minimum Lock-Up Period After Which You Can Take Qualified Withdrawals	Contribution can be withdrawn anytime. To withdraw earnings as well, account must be open for 5 years.	None.	Some states may impose limits from 3 years and up.	None.
How Will Your Child's Financial Aid be Affected?	No impact.	Money considered a student asset, meaning less financial aid than if were considered a parental asset.	Currently the money is considered a parental asset so it will reduce financial aid but not by as much as if asset were considered a student asset. Of course all of this chould change and it is subject to the will of the educational institution in question.	Money considered a student asset meaning less financial aid than if it were a parental asset.

Websites/Publications/Services

We generally don't recommend many websites because of the alarming rates at which they either disappear or begin to charge fees. The websites we do mention in the book are free; only a few require any type of registration. To see updates, you can check www.teeenvestor.com/top_websites.htm.

CHAPTER 1
Websites for Managing Your Finances

Securities & Exchange Commission	www.sec.gov
American Savings Education Council	www.asec.org
Federal Consumer Information Center	www.pueblo.gsa.gov
Treasury Direct	www.publicdebt.treas.gov
The Investor's Clearinghouse	www.investoreducation.org
Federal Deposit Insurance	www.fdic.gov

CHAPTER 6
Websites for Credit Union Information

National Credit Union Administration	www.ncua.gov
Credit Unions Online	www.creditunionsonline.com

CHAPTER 7
Websites for Bank Rate Comparisons
Bankrate.com   www.bankrate.com
Gomez Advisors   www.gomez.com

Websites for Credit Union Information
National Credit Union Administration   www.ncua.gov
Credit Unions Online   www.creditunionsonline.com

Traditional Banks
Citibank   www.citibank.com
Bank of America   www.bankofamerica.com
Chase Manhattan Bank   www.chase.com
Wells Fargo   www.wellsfargo.com
Fleet Bank   www.fleet.com

Internet-Only Banks
EtradeBank   www.etradebank.com
NetBank   www.netbank.com
First Internet Bank of Indiana   www.firstib.com
Pcbanker.com   www.pcbanker.com

Bank for Teenvestors
Young Americans Bank   www.theyoungamericans.org

CHAPTER 8
Educational Websites for Beginners
Teenvestor.com   www.teenvestor.com
TeenAnalyst   www.teenanalyst.com
The Motley Fool   www.fool.com
Investopedia   www.investopedia.com
Morningstar   www.morningstar.com
NASD   www.investor.nasd.com
SmartMoney   www.smartmoney.com
InvestorGuide.com   www.investorguide.com
The Vanguard Group   www.vanguard.com
Mutual Fund Education Alliance   www.mfea.com
New York Stock Exchange   www.nyse.com
About   stocks.about.com,
mutualfunds.about.com

Stock Indices

The Teenvestor Index	www.teenvestor.com/indices.htm
The Dow	www.djindexes.com
The S&P 500	www.spglobaldata.com
The NASDAQ	www.nasdaq.com
The NASDAQ 100	www.nasdaq.com
The Russell 3000	www.russell.com
The Wilshire 5000	www.willshire.com
TSX Composite Index (Canada)	www.tse.com
FTSE 100 (United Kingdom)	www.ftse.com
Hang Seng (Hong Kong)	www.his.com.hk
Nikkei 225 (Japan)	www.nni.nikkei.co.jp
DAX (Germany)	www.deutsche-boerse.com

CHAPTER 9

Current Business News Websites

CBS MarketWatch	www.cbsmarketwatch.com
CNBC	www.cnbc.com
CNN Money	money.cnn.com
The Street	www.thestreet.com
New York Times	www.nytimes.com
Bloomberg	www.bloomberg.com
Los Angeles Times	www.latimes.com
BusinessWeek Online	www.businessweek.com
Fortune	www.fortune.com

Research Websites

The SEC	www.sec.gov
Microsoft's Money Central	www.moneycentral.msn.com
Multex Investor	www.multexinvestor.com
Hoover's	www.hoovers.com
Smart Money	www.smartmoney.com
Morningstar	www.morningstar.com
Netstockdirect	www.netstockdirect.com
Freeedgar	www.freeedgar.com
The Online Investor	www.theonlineinvestor.com

Historical Stock Prices

BigCharts.com	www.bigcharts.com
Yahoo!Finance	finance.yahoo.com
ClearStation	www.clearstation.com

Websites for Dummy Portfolios
Quicken	www.quicken.com
Yahoo!Finance	finance.yahoo.com
Wall Street City	www.wallstreetcity.com
ClearStation	www.clearstation.com
Microsoft's Money Central	www.moneycentral.msn.com
Lycos	finance.lycos.com
SmartMoney	www.smartmoney.com

Affordable Online Brokers
Firstrade	www.firstrade.com
Trading Direct	www.tradingdirect.com
Scottrade	www.scottrade.com
Mydiscountbroker.com	www.mydiscountbroker.com
BrokerageAmerica	www.brokerageamerica.com
TD Waterhouse	www.tdwaterhouse.com
Etrade	www.etrade.com
Ameritrade	www.ameritrade.com

CHAPTER 11
Direct Investing Plan Information
Netstockdirect	www.netstockdirect.com
DirectInvesting.com	www.directinvesting.com
Drip Advisor	www.dripadvisor.com
Equiserve	www.equiserve.com
Mellon Investor Services	www.melloninvestor.com

Services to Help You Register Shares
Money Paper's Temper Enrollment Service	www.moneypaper.com (800-295-2550)
NAIC's "Own a Share of America"	www.better-investing.org
First Share	www.firstshare.com

CHAPTER 12
Websites for Mutual Fund Information
Morningstar	www.morningstar.com
Money Central	www.moneycentral.msn.com
The Vanguard Group	www.vanguard.com
The Motley Fool	www.fool.com
About	mutualfunds.about.com
The Mutual Fund Education Alliance	www.mfea.com

CHAPTER 13
Major No-Load Funds

Vanguard 500 Index (VFINX)	800-871-3879
	www.vanguard.com
USAA S&P 500 Index (USSPX)	800-382-8722
	www.usaa.com
Scudder S&P 500 Index (SCPIX)	800-728-3337
	www.scudder.com
T. Rowe Price Equity Index 500 (PREIX)	800-225-5132
	www.troweprice.com
Schwab S&P 500 Fund (SWPIX)	877-488-6762
	www.schwab.com
T. Rowe Price Total Market Index (POMIX)	800-225-5132
	www.troweprice.com
Vanguard Total Stock Market Index (VTSMX)	800-871-3879
	www.vanguard.com
TIAA-CREF Equity Index Fund	800-223-1200
	www.tiaacref.com
Vanguard Small-Cap Index (NAESX)	800-871-3879
	www.vanguard.com

Teenvestor-Friendly Funds

Liberty Young Investor Z (SRYIX)	800-426-3750
	www.libertyfunds.com
USAA First Start Growth (UFSGX)	800-235-8377
	www.usaa.com
Invesco (FLRFX)	800-525-8085
	www.invesco.com
American Express IDS New Dimensions (INDBX)	800-437-4332
	www.americanexpress.com
Monetta (MLCEX)	800-Monetta
	www.monetta.com

CHAPTER 14
Websites for Exchange Traded Funds

American Stock Exchange	www.amex.com
Barklays Global Investors	www.ishares.com
Nuveen Investments	www.etfconnect.com
NASDAQ	www.nasdaq.com
Morningstar	www.morningstar.com
State Street Global Advisors	www.streettracks.com

CHAPTER 15
College Savings Plan Information

College Savings Plans Network	www.collegesavings.com
Savingforcollege.com	www.savingforcollege.com

CHAPTER 16
College Savings Plan Information

College Savings Plans Network	www.collegesavings.com
Savingforcollege.com	www.savingforcollege.com

College Savings Plan Information

Finaid	www.finaid.com
Collegeboard.com	www.collegeboard.com
Department of Education	www.ed.gov, www.fafsa.ed.gov

State Treasurers' Websites

National Association of State Treasurers (for websites of all U.S. State Treasurers who handle college savings plans)	www.nast.net

Information on College Savings Plans

Kiplinger's	www.kiplinger.com
Mutual Funds Magazine	www.mutual-funds.com
CNNfn	www.cnnfn.com
Forbes	www.forbes.com
USAToday	www.usatoday.com
SmartMoney	www.smartmoney.com/college
Collegeboard.com	www.collegeboard.com

CHAPTERS 17 AND 19
Information on Coverdell Educational Savings Accounts

Internal Revenue Service (Publication 590)	www.irs.gov

Information on IRAs

Internal Revenue Service (Publication 590)	www.irs.gov
The Motley Fool	www.fool.com
SmartMoney	www.smartmoney.com

CHAPTER 21
Savings Bonds

Savings Bonds Direct	www.savingsbonds.gov

Index